W9-CQS-236

Shakespeare's Consuls, Cardinals, and Kings

Ex Libris

Prof. Sam Cundiff Saunders

VERO NIHIL VERIUS

IGNORANCE IS CRIMINAL, ESPECIALLY

WHEN IT IS VOLUNTARY.

Dr. Samuel Johnson

KNOWLEDGE, WITHOUT THOUGHT,

IS USELESS.

AND THOUGHT WITHOUT KNOWLEDGE

IS FUTILE, OR PERILOUS.

The Twelfth Analect of Cunfucius

Shakespeare's Consuls, Cardinals, and Kings

The Real History behind the Plays

DICK RILEY
Illustrations by Jessa Lowell

To Rochester and his "Maxwell" who follows the geological evidence of J. Harlan Bretz as well as the Shakespeare enigma

[signature]

continuum

NEW YORK • LONDON

2008

The Continuum International Publishing Group Inc
80 Maiden Lane, New York, NY 10038

The Continuum International Publishing Group Ltd
The Tower Building, 11 York Road, London SE1 7NX

www.continuumbooks.com

Copyright © 2008 by Dick Riley

All rights reserved. No part of this book may be reproduced, stored in a
retrieval system, or transmitted, in any form or by any means, electronic,
mechanical, photocopying, recording, or otherwise, without the written
permission of the publishers.

Printed in the United States of America on 50% postconsumer waste recycled
paper

Library of Congress Cataloging-in-Publication Data
    Riley, Dick.
        Shakespeare's consuls, cardinals, and kings : the real history behind the
    plays/Dick Riley; illustrations by Jessa Lowell.
            p. cm.
        Includes bibliographical references and index.
        ISBN-13: 978-0-8264-1880-7 (pbk. : alk. paper)
        ISBN-10: 0-8264-1880-5 (pbk. : alk. paper)
        1. Shakespeare, William, 1564-1616–Knowledge–History. 2. Shakespeare,
    William, 1564-1616–Histories. 3. Shakespeare, William, 1564-1616–
    Characters–Kings and rulers. 4. Historical drama, English–History
    and criticism. 5. Political plays, English–History and criticism. 6. Great
    Britain–History–1066-1687–Historiography. 7. Great Britain–In literature.
    8. Rome–Historiography. 9. Rome–In literature. 10. Kings and rulers in
    literature.
    I. Title.
    PR3014.R55 2008
    822.3'3—dc22

CONTENTS

Introduction

William Shakespeare brings history to life.

On Shakespeare's stage, stories hundreds or even thousands of years old appear before our eyes, thrusting the events of the past into our own day. Thanks to Shakespeare, we hear the Roman leader Marc Antony speaking over the body of the slain Julius Caesar; we laugh at the Elizabethan comedy of low manners in the person of Sir John Falstaff; we get to watch as Richard III schemes his way to power over the bodies of friends and family members.

A deeper knowledge of history may not be strictly necessary for us to enjoy these plays. But understanding more of the background of Marc Antony, the Elizabethan economic realities faced by Falstaff and his fictional crew, or even the Tudor propaganda campaign against the memory of Richard III, can provide new perspectives on the plays and give us deeper insights into the characters Shakespeare has drawn for us.

We know, for example, that Marc Antony's speech so inflamed the Roman masses that they drove Caesar's noble assassins out of the city, setting into motion the civil war that occupies much of *Julius Caesar* and *Antony and Cleopatra*. Shakespeare's play *Julius Caesar* presents us with the bluff, plainspoken Marc Antony; but Shakespeare's sources show us a subtler character, one who dined with Caesar's assassins after Caesar's murder, persuading them that he meant them no harm, to the point where they permitted him to give Caesar's funeral oration – with the results that we all know. (Shakespeare also much improved Marc Antony's speech, at least when we compare it to the original version as handed down to us by the Roman historian Dio Cassius.)

Sir John Falstaff may have been a fictional character in the *Henry IV* plays, but his personal extravagances had a real-life resonance for the working-class playgoers who occupied the standing room in front of the Elizabethan stage. Modern audiences can still enjoy Sir John's antics, but we can get a new insight into his lifestyle by knowing that the bill for a single dinner found in his pocket would have been enough to feed a contemporary workingman in Shakespeare's audience for a month – something the "groundlings" would have immediately understood.

Richard III has gone down in history as one of England's most villainous kings. But later scholarship has given us a fuller picture of Richard, and some experts think it possible that he may not have committed his most famous crime – the murder of his nephews, the princes in the Tower.

Realizing what Shakespeare left out of the stories he tells can also give us a useful insight into what remains. For many modern students of political science, the most memorable incident of King John's reign is the signing of Magna Carta, the charter that limited royal power. Magna Carta, however, gets not even a passing reference in Shakespeare's play about this king's reign because in Shakespeare's time Magna Carta was not regarded as much of a political milestone. It was only during parliament's power struggles with later kings – decades after Shakespeare's death – that Magna Carta was seized upon as an important historical model.

Shakespeare's Sources

While Shakespeare may have read widely in available histories to find plots to dramatize, it is clear that several writers served as his primary sources. For *Julius Caesar* and *Antony and Cleopatra* the most important source was Plutarch, a Greek historian of the Roman Empire who wrote around the turn of the first century CE. Plutarch tried to link his native Greek culture with that of the Romans, who by his time had dominated the eastern Mediterranean for decades. In his *Lives of the Noble Greeks and Romans*, he sought parallels between the biographies of notable Greek and Roman leaders who had similar natures or who faced similar problems. Other sources for the Roman plays may have included Suetonius, an official of the Roman Emperor Hadrian who wrote *The Twelve Caesars*; and Dio Cassius, a Roman senator and historian who lived around the turn of the second century CE.

For the English plays, Shakespeare relied heavily on the *Chronicles of England, Scotland and Ireland*, which is credited to Raphael Holinshed, although other writers were also involved; and Edward Hall's *Union of the Two Noble and Illustrious Families of Lancaster and York*. Shakespeare also occasionally used elements he found in the work of other Elizabethan dramatists, such as the anonymous play *The Famous Victories of Henry V*.

Most discussions of the "history" plays begin with the observation that Shakespeare was a dramatist, not a historian. But the truth is that like any writer of history, Shakespeare weighed the information from his sources, determined which provided the most useful account, and tried to make the past a visible reality for his audience. He viewed his sources as inspirations, and he never felt himself bound by them. To meet the needs of popular drama – and Shakespeare as a dramatist was first and foremost a commercial artist – he telescoped events, changed locations, and combined characters. But his agenda was aesthetic, not partisan, and his plays are as vital today as they were four centuries ago because they reflect the human reality we all share.

How to Use This Book

Shakespeare's Consuls, Cardinals, and Kings is meant to be a companion volume to these plays. Each chapter describes the historical context for the events of a play (or series of plays), then goes through the work, pointing out how Shakespeare used – and often tailored – the historical record to suit the needs of the stage. I've also tried to point out where there is substantial disagreement among Shakespeare's sources or later historians about a character or incident.

Most people encounter these works in individual productions rather than as a continuous series, so each chapter begins with a certain amount of background, identifying plot details or characters from the previous play in the cycle, where appropriate. Under the circumstances, a certain amount of repetition is unavoidable, but I hope to have kept it to a minimum. The rest of each chapter is designed to take the reader through the play or plays act by act to help explain the context for events or to provide an additional point of view.

The selected plays are certainly not the only works Shakespeare derived from historical sources; the plot of *Macbeth* (and elements of other plays) can be found in Holinshed, whereas Plutarch was clearly the source for *Coriolanus*. But I have tried to focus on those works where a broader knowledge of the historical period is most useful, and where there are multiple sources upon which to rely.

ACKNOWLEDGMENTS

I want to thank a number of individuals and institutions that were helpful in the process of writing this book. They include: the staffs of the New York and White Plains public libraries; James Ryan of Dominican College of Blauvelt, New York, who shared with me his insights into the structure of the plays, particularly *Julius Caesar*; and my editor, Evander Lomke, for his continuing support of this project.

My most important supporters, of this and so many other undertakings, have been my family: my wife, Marcia and my children, Ian and Jessa. I will be forever grateful for their help and understanding.

1

"In servile fearfulness"

Julius Caesar

Shakespeare's play is an account of the plot to assassinate Julius Caesar and the subsequent deaths of his principal assailants. But the story told by the play is actually a small part in the much larger drama that was the late Roman republic. Caesar's murder was but one of many in a period marked by class struggle, partisan violence, and civil war. The events dramatized in *Julius Caesar* and its sequel, *Antony and Cleopatra*, represent milestones in the long story of how the Roman Republic, a form of government that had endured for centuries, became the Roman Empire.

In the century or so before the play begins, Rome, a small city-state with grand ambitions, absorbed many of the other cities and cultures of the Italian peninsula. It then expanded across the Mediterranean, eliminating its main seagoing opponent, Carthage, and extending its power into the populous, affluent, and cosmopolitan cities of the Greek-speaking east.

That expansion was, at best, a mixed blessing for Roman society. Because of these new alliances and conquests trade expanded, tax revenues and wealth grew, and slaves poured into Roman society in unprecedented numbers. Taking advantage of the fact that many small farmers were away for extended periods fighting – the Roman citizen army at the time was largely made up of small landholders – the wealthy bought up their farms and combined them into large-scale operations employing huge gangs of slaves.

Industrial farming made agricultural production more efficient and reduced the price of the grain that was a staple of the Roman diet. The downside was that returning soldiers had no farms to go back to, so they swelled the ranks of the un- and underemployed masses in the cities, Rome in particular. This class, once the backbone of a traditional agricultural society, became a turbulent element in urban politics. Meanwhile, because of the downward pressure on wages from slave workers, the artisan class also lost ground economically. It seemed to many Roman citizens that the rich got richer while the middle class and the poor grew steadily worse off.

In the decades leading up to Caesar's death, two political points of view evolved. The *populares* stood for debt relief, land for the dispossessed, a public-works program for the unemployed, and other policies that were designed to help Rome's working and middle classes. As might be expected, their agenda found considerable support among those groups, although there were reformist elements in the Senate and the wealthy classes who sympathized with these goals.

Arrayed against them were the *optimates*, roughly translated as "the best people." This group included the old guard of the Senate, landed families, merchants who had prospered as Rome's reach expanded, and a significant number of people of all classes who had internalized Rome's self-definition as a state without a king.

The conflict between optimates and populares did not emerge with Caesar. It had been the catalyst for the rise of Caesar's spiritual antecedents, the Gracchi brothers, in the last part of the second century BCE. The Gracchi were of noble birth but took up the popular cause, and both were eventually murdered. More recently, Caesar's uncle, Marius, a famous general, identified with the populares and brought his legions to Rome to take over the city in 87 BCE, putting to death his political opponents. Marius's former deputy and longtime rival, Sulla, reversed this trend in 82 BCE when *his* legions took over Rome, undid many of Marius's reforms, and launched a reign of terror that cost the lives of hundreds – perhaps thousands – of Romans. Caesar, as Marius's nephew, was a logical target of Sulla's death squads. He escaped because of his relative youth and because he was related not only to Marius but also to Sulla. (The Roman leadership class was not large.)

In adulthood, Caesar opted for the populares, while the noted general Pompey leaned toward the cause of the optimates. Pompey had been one of Sulla's subordinates, won a number of important military victories on his own, and for a time was a political ally of Caesar. In fact, Pompey and Caesar were two members of the political troika known as the

First Triumvirate, essentially an informal three-way agreement to govern Rome in 60 BCE by bypassing the Senate and other institutions of the Republic. Pompey, though six years Caesar's senior, was also for some period his son-in-law. But as the Roman historian Plutarch dryly notes, "Pompey could bide no equal, nor Caesar a superior," and their alliance fell apart after the death of Julia, Caesar's daughter and Pompey's wife.

In the Roman republic, military achievement was a virtual requirement for the highest offices, so ambitious politicians took it upon themselves to become generals. Pompey already had a distinguished military reputation. Caesar burnished his own with victories over the Gauls and Germans, keeping the Senate and Rome informed of his success through the letters that were later collected as his commentaries on the Gallic Wars.

Then, in 47 BCE, while locked in a dispute with Pompey and the Senate, Caesar and one of his legions crossed the Rubicon – a stream in northern Italy that marked the northern border of the Republic. Outmaneuvering his opponents, he advanced to and occupied Rome in a virtually bloodless coup.

Most of the members of the Senate's political faction opposed to Caesar beat a strategic retreat. Led by Pompey, they languished for some time in southern Italy, then took ship for the east to raise troops. Caesar eventually followed them and, in the Battle of Pharsalus against a far superior force, routed them. Pompey fled to Egypt but was murdered on his arrival. His sons continued the contest, and Caesar eventually went to

Spain to defeat them. It was from this campaign that Caesar has returned as Shakespeare's drama begins.

The Challenge of Governing Rome

Our image of Roman politics is shaped largely by our impression of the Empire as a centrally administered operation headed by a more or less absolute ruler. This view, not completely accurate for the Empire, is particularly misleading in the case of the Republic. In Caesar's time, the contest between populares and optimates was to some extent a struggle to win – or at least to manipulate – not the influence of the Senate or the Republic's officers, but rather the popular will that, in the last analysis, governed the state.

Only free adult males who possessed certain property qualifications actually were citizens of Rome. But their numbers were still substantial. These citizens voted on most of the major questions of the day and elected candidates for the hugely confusing superstructure of Roman offices with overlapping and contradictory responsibilities and powers. The most prestigious annual offices were those of consul, of which there were two, specifically so that one could overrule the other if there was any disagreement over policy. There were tribunes, including some known as "tribunes of the people," that could overturn the rulings of the consuls if they thought the rulings hurt the peoples' interests. There were a host of other positions, including praetors, who oversaw government accounts, and aediles, who sponsored the gladiatorial and other games that were a staple of public life and a great way to build popular support for a run for higher office.

There were three assemblies or convocations to which Roman citizens could belong: the comitia centuriata, which voted on war and peace and elected consuls; the comitia curiata, which empowered magistrates; and the comitia tributa, which elected tribunes of the people.

It was not exactly one man/one vote. Groups within the comitia voted as blocs, and it was fairly simple for the most organized, richest, or otherwise most powerful groups to carry issues and elect candidates to the offices of the Republic. The buying and selling of votes became pervasive and was an essential campaign strategy for ambitious politicians.

The Senate had originated as a gathering of magistrates and an advisory – not legislative – council to the officers elected by the comitia. Senate resolutions had to be confirmed by the assemblies before going into effect. At the height of its prestige, the Senate, dominated by wealthy interests, could rely on the comitia to rubber-stamp its decrees. But when the situation of the common people became dire, the comitia could and did take matters into their own hands, ignoring the Senate's wishes.

Preserving this structure and its underlying rights was the stated goal of many of the conspirators against Caesar, who saw the political system threatened by the possibility that – given his popularity – he would become a king. The last monarchy, the Tarquins, had been driven from the city nearly four hundred years before, but the legends of their tyranny had grown rather than diminished over time. It was a point of considerable pride to many Romans that they, in effect, governed themselves, rather than relied on a monarch. So reluctant were Romans under the Republic to suffer one-man rule that they permitted the appointment of a dictator (that's where we get the word) only in times of crisis and then only for a short and predetermined period, although the process could be and was manipulated by Sulla and Caesar, among others.

Setting the Stage for *Julius Caesar*

As Shakespeare's play opens, Roman society has endured years of civil war between the adherents of Caesar and Pompey, the climax of decades of unrest since the deaths of the Gracchi brothers and the proscriptions of Marius and Sulla. In a departure from Roman practice, Caesar had not followed his victories with the execution of his political opponents; instead he granted them the all-but-universal amnesty that was a constant theme in Caesar's life. (Among his assassins were nobles who had actively fought against him and who had been permitted not only to live, but often had been entrusted with important offices.)

Having conciliated some of his opponents, beaten and largely forgiven others, Caesar was contemplating undertaking a series of public works, such as vastly improving the Roman port down the Tiber River at Ostia, a project that would benefit Rome's merchant class while relieving unemployment. And far from planning to run the Republic with an iron hand, he was about to embark on a campaign that would have been the capstone to his military and political career – an invasion of Parthia, the eastern empire that had a few years before humbled Roman arms by defeating an invading force of legions under the general Crassus.

Yet as the play begins, noble members of the anti-Caesarian faction – Marullus and Flavius – berate a crowd of workmen who have abandoned their tasks to welcome Caesar back from his internecine wars. What prisoners does Caesar bring back "to grace in captive bonds his chariot wheels?" asks the patrician Marullus. He knows, as do the workmen, that the traditional victory parade where the winning general rode through the streets with important captives beside his chariot was an honor granted only to a general who defeated foreign foes, not his own countrymen.

Referring to the proletarians' previous enthusiasms, Marullus reminds them that when they watched Pompey's chariot in previous victory parades, "have you not made an universal shout that Tiber trembled underneath her banks." Shooing the workmen away, Flavius vows to "drive the vulgar from the streets" while removing from Caesar's statues the garlands and decorations placed by his adherents that might suggest royalty and encourage an ambition that would "keep us all in servile fearfulness."

Shakespeare's language choice reflects the class conflict. Marullus repeatedly uses "thou" in his address to the workmen. Modern English has lost this distinction (still preserved in Romance languages) between "you" the formal second person, and "thou" used with family members or to address persons of lower rank. The distinction would not have been lost on Shakespeare's own working-class audience, the groundlings in front of the stage, who also would have enjoyed the fact that the workmen, while pretending to be respectful, clearly get the better of their social superiors.

The Lupercal

In the play, the conspirators – not yet formed to their purpose – hear of an incident at the festival of the Lupercal, where Marc Antony, Caesar's longtime aide and deputy, offered Caesar a kind of crown in front of the assembled people, a crown "which he did thrice refuse." But, as Casca, no friend of Caesar, reports, "I think he would fain have had it." Many historians, even those sympathetic with Caesar, assume that the incident was a bit of street theater organized by Caesar and Marc Antony to test popular support for a crown for Caesar. (Shakespeare places the Lupercal shortly before the ides of March, when in fact it was weeks before.)

Shakespeare makes Cassius the center of the conspiracy and his brother-in-law Brutus the first target for conversion. Cassius was a veteran soldier who had survived the ill-starred Parthian campaign of Crassus. Brutus claimed descent from the Brutus who led the opposition to the Tarquin monarchy. Although Caesar had a relationship of long standing with Brutus's mother, Brutus had rejected Caesar and joined Pompey's faction because he saw Pompey as defending the Republic. He took Pompey's side against Caesar in the battle of Pharsalus (as did Cassius); afterward, Caesar was reportedly overjoyed to find that Brutus had survived the battle despite Pompey's defeat.

Not all historians agree that Brutus was so unalloyed a hero as the play would make him, but his support was clearly a key to the conspiracy, and his insistence that Marc Antony remain unharmed was a mistake that helped undo the conspiracy's apparent success.

The Night Before

Religion and the spiritual world were a constant concern of the Romans, who believed – as did Shakespeare's audiences – that divine or otherwordly forces expressed themselves through signs, portents, and extraordinary natural phenomena. There is also significance in Shakespeare setting the conspiracy at night. In most of Roman as well as English history, the narrow, tangled streets of urban areas were unpoliced and dangerous after dark; until the nineteenth century, most cities had neither a regular police force nor effective street lighting. Roman dinner parties were held not at night but in the afternoon, so that guests could find their way home while there was still daylight.

Confirming the secret nature of their nocturnal errand, the conspirators never actually enter Brutus's house, where they might be seen by guests or servants, but instead come and go through the gate in the garden, meeting in an open space where, under most circumstances, the family would not go at night. Shakespeare has Brutus agree to join the conspiracy not in a dialogue with the conspirators but rather in an offstage conversation with Cassius. When the two rejoin the group gathered in the garden, the choice has been made, and it becomes a question not of whether Caesar shall be assassinated, but how and when.

Left out of the conspiracy was the greatest orator of the day, Marcus Tullius Cicero, a member of the conservative faction who had a substantial following and whom all thought would be sympathetic to the conspirators' cause. Shakespeare has Brutus tell the other plotters that Cicero "will never follow anything that other men begin," but Plutarch's judgment is a good deal more pointed, saying that Cicero "was a man whom they loved dearly and trusted best; for they were afraid that he being a coward by nature, he would quite turn and alter their purpose."

Caesar's House

Just as important as natural phenomena to the Romans were dreams, their recall, and their interpretation. They are also a recurring theme in Shakespeare, here getting their first exposure in this play, as Caesar's wife is troubled not only by the signs and portents but by her own dreams.

Much of this material, including the fears of Caesar's wife, was taken from Plutarch and expanded. The visit of Decius to Caesar's house to bring him to the Senate meeting is a direct lift from Plutarch, as is Decius's reinterpretation of the auguries that troubled Calpurnia and Caesar. The dramatic gesture of all the conspirators conducting Caesar to the Senate meeting appears to have been Shakespeare's creation

– according to Plutarch, the conspirators other than Decius met at the house of Cassius and went from there to the Senate meeting to await Caesar's arrival.

The message from Artemidorus about the conspiracy is also from Plutarch, who merely says that Caesar was too busy to read it, rather than Shakespeare's bravura statement that "what touches Caesar" he would consider last.

Caesar has often been assumed to have met his fate in the Senate house on the Capitol, but, in fact, the Senate meeting on the Ides of March was held in the portico of Pompey's theater, outside the city walls on the Campus Martius. According to the historian Dio Cassius (a Roman official who lived from about 155 CE to 229 CE), the conspirators, thinking they might need help, used the theatrical location as an excuse to station gladiators nearby, under the fiction that they were to perform in the theater later. (There is no record that they were needed.)

The actual details of the attack follow Plutarch fairly closely, although "et tu, brute," Caesar's final statement to Brutus, is not mentioned. Dio Cassius reports that some have said Caesar uttered these words, and the historian Suetonius echoes that possibility, although he also adds that if Caesar said it, it might well have been in Greek, commonly spoken by educated Romans, and in that language would have been "Kai su, teknon," or "You, too, my son." The latter construction, along with Caesar's well-known concern for Brutus and his relationship with Brutus's mother, Servilia, fueled speculation that Brutus was Caesar's son by Servilia. The fact that Caesar was only fifteen years older than Brutus, and his relationship with Servilia was known to date from sometime after Brutus's birth, makes this unlikely although not impossible.

Historians agree that all the conspirators made sure to take part in the actual attack, and that Caesar died at the foot of Pompey's statue in a building that his old antagonist had commissioned to burnish his own reputation. The inherent irony was lost on none of the witnesses.

After the Assassination

Shakespeare telescopes and rearranges the historical account of the aftermath of Caesar's death. In the play, Antony meets with the conspirators over Caesar's body, convinces them of his peaceful intentions, and extracts their permission to have a eulogy and official burial for Caesar. (In the usual order of Roman political assassinations, the body of the deceased would be dumped into the Tiber.)

In Plutarch's account, after the assassination the conspirators walked to the Capitol, bloody swords in hand, and announced to the marketplace what they had done. Given Brutus's reputation, his statement was received with respect by the audience, which then began to protest when another assassin spoke to attack Caesar. Sensing the tenor of the crowd, Brutus and the other conspirators withdrew to the safety of the Capitol. Caesar's body lay for hours in front of Pompey's statue before his household slaves came to carry it back to his house.

The Senate met again the next day in the temple of the goddess Tellus and resolved, in effect, that the conspirators should be pardoned. That night, members of the conspiracy and the Caesarian party dined together. It was at still another meeting of the Senate on the following day that Antony received permission to have a funeral for Caesar, an idea strongly opposed by Cassius but supported by Brutus. Such ceremonies, with orations about the deeds of the deceased, were commonly made for famous Romans, and Brutus was eager to add what air of normalcy he could to the situation.

According to Plutarch, Caesar's will leaving his funds to the people and his lands near the city for a park was made public before Antony's funeral oration. (Shakespeare puts the news in Antony's speech.) The oration itself, given only passing mention by Plutarch, was apparently much improved by Shakespeare. It is hard now to find the drama and passion in the version quoted extensively by the Roman historian Dio Cassius.

Instead of "Friends, Romans, countrymen," the Dio Cassius version includes a long opening by Antony,

> . . . it is requisite that I
> should deliver a twofold address, one as the man
> set down as his "heir" (actually he was more like a
> guardian of Caesar's estate) and one in my capacity
> as magistrate (he was Caesar's colleague in the con-
> sulship that year) and I must not omit anything that
> ought to be spoken, but must mention the things
> which the whole people would have spoken with
> one tongue if they could speak with one voice. . . . I
> feel sure that you will not judge my goodwill by the
> feebleness of my words, but will supply from my
> zeal whatever is lacking in that respect.

Nevertheless, even in Dio Cassius's account, the speech and the display of Caesar's bloody garments were enough to inflame the crowd, whose members gathered up all the wooden furniture and artifacts in the area and created a funeral pyre for Caesar. They then attempted to attack the houses of Caesar's killers, where they ran into the unfortunate Cinna, a poet and friend of Caesar's whose similarity of name to Cinna the conspirator was enough to lead to his death. Alarmed by the reaction of the people, the conspirators withdrew from Rome.

Most historians believe the conspirators had no real plan in the wake of the assassination, assuming that the Republic would reassert itself. In fact, the Republic was up for grabs, and one of the contestants for power was just coming on to the scene – Octavian, Caesar's grandnephew, who was named his heir in the great man's will. In the play Octavian is said to be just outside Rome at the time of the assassination, but in reality he was in the Balkans. He hurried to Rome, sped on by the realization that as Caesar's heir he would either have to take a leading place in Roman society or risk being eliminated by other candidates for Caesar's legacy.

Shakespeare makes no real attempt to recount what happened next. With the conspirators having left for the eastern provinces, Antony remained consul and ended up breaking with the Senate. The Senatorial opposition was led by Cicero, who began to believe that Antony was as dangerous to the republic as Caesar had been and who denounced Antony in a series of bitter speeches now known as the Philippics. Leaders loyal to the Senate ended up fighting Antony in Gaul, including Lepidus, whose legions, veterans of Caesar's wars, soon defected to Antony's side.

Meanwhile, Octavian, although only a teenager in a society that valued maturity, played upon his status as Caesar's heir. Calling himself Julius Caesar, he emerged as a significant player in the confused political situation. Part of his success came about because Cicero had sponsored him as a counterweight to Antony. But when the Senate refused Octavian's demands for the consulship and funds for his legions, he used his political and military clout to take control of the city and have himself elected consul.

The Triumvirs

Octavian, Antony, and Lepidus created a somewhat shaky partnership in 43 BCE in the Second Triumvirate. They were essentially dictators, assuming legislative and executive powers, although they retained some of the appurtenances of republican government, including deferring on some issues to the Senate, which they enlarged with their supporters.

The triumvirs also took up the brutal political tradition of the proscriptions of Marius and Sulla. A bloodbath followed, with thousands of men executed by death squads, some of whom were given up by their friends or even relatives. The play makes passing reference (act 4, scene 1) to a meeting of Octavian, Antony, and Lepidus where the proscription lists were drawn up. Some victims died because of their history of political opposition, others because the triumvirs were desperate for money to pay their legions (the property of the proscribed was confiscated by the government).

Many historians see Antony as the principal player in the bloodshed. Lepidus, according to Dio Cassius, "was not inexorable" and let some of the proscribed escape, while Octavian, because of his youth, had few personal enemies. But Antony had a reputation for anger and a taste for vengeance. It was routine for the executioners to bring back the heads of their victims to prove they deserved their pay, and Antony, according to Dio Cassius, "always viewed their heads, even if he was eating, and sated himself to the fullest extent on this most unholy and pitiable sight." After he had Cicero executed, Antony had the orator's head nailed to the rostra, the public speaking post from which Cicero once so often denounced Antony.

Powers in the East

The Roman sphere of influence was effectively divided. Brutus and Cassius were, for all intents and purposes, the governors of the east. They sat in different provinces – Brutus had taken time out in Athens to study Greek philosophy – and they used the wealth of their provinces to raise legions, keeping from Rome the substantial taxes the east traditionally paid into the treasury.

Of the disagreements between Brutus and Cassius dramatized in the play, Dio Cassius says, "all the suspicions which they were harboring against each other as the result of calumnius talk . . . they brought forward and discussed with each other in privacy,

and after becoming reconciled again they hastened
into Macedonia." Plutarch reports that "they two
alone . . . began first to expostulate, then to dispute
hotly, and accuse each other; and finally were so
transported into passion as to fall to hard words,
and at last burst out into tears." The disagreement
between Brutus and Cassius had to do with money,
money that was primarily spent on raising troops and
naval forces to deal with Marc Antony and Octavian.
The Caesarians, knowing they could not be secure
without solving the long-term threat to their power
posed by Brutus and Cassius in the east, raised their
own legions and took ship to settle the issue on their
enemies' ground.

The battle at Philippi was a good deal more drawn
out than the play indicates. The first phase involved
an attack by Antony on troops of Cassius that carried
on into Cassius's headquarters. Believing wrongly
that he and his allies were overrun, Cassius committed
suicide. In fact, the attack on his camp had fallen back,
and in the meantime Brutus had successfully attacked
Octavian's camp, forcing Octavian to flee.

The second phase began about three weeks later.
The remaining forces of Caesar's assassins, led by
Brutus, had a strong ally in Sextus Pompey (Pompey's
son and as such a natural ally of Caesar's assassins),
who controlled the sea lanes and theoretically could
have starved out Marc Antony and Octavian's forces.
However, Brutus joined battle, according to Dio
Cassius, in part because he feared defections from
his forces to those of the Caesarians. Brutus was
decisively defeated and committed suicide. Antony,
as in the play, covered the body with his own cloak

and honored him as the only one of the conspirators who fought for the idea of the Republic rather than personal animosity or ambition.

Republican sentiment was far from extinguished, but the republican cause was effectively lost. Thousands of survivors from the legions of Brutus and Cassius enlisted in the forces of Antony and Octavian.

The Stories Not Told

The play touches on many important incidents in the fall of the Republic, but may be most interesting for two stories it makes no real attempt to tell – those of Cleopatra and Octavian.

After Pompey's defeat and subsequent murder, Caesar had gone to Egypt, where he got involved in a dynastic struggle on the side of the teenage queen, Cleopatra, and ended up in a personal as well as political relationship. He lingered long enough with his eastern mistress that he was criticized even by his supporters for dallying, and in Dio Cassius's version of the funeral oration, Antony takes pains to say that Caesar's later military victory proved that he "had not become weaker in Alexandria and had not delayed there out of voluptuousness." Cleopatra attributed the birth of her son to Caesar, and named him Caesarion. She eventually followed him to Rome and was there when Caesar was assassinated.

Octavian, relying on the heritage of his uncle's name and his own highly developed political sense, maneuvered his way through the thicket of Roman politics and war. He not only survived, but eventually ruled Rome alone as Caesar Augustus, the first great leader of the Roman Empire.

Caesar's Character and Ambition

As long as historians write about this period they will continue to disagree about the real impetus for Caesar's actions. Was he a demagogue who embraced the popular cause because he saw it as the only route to the top? Or was he truly ambitious for the public good and saw his own elevation as Rome's best hope for the future? Writers of his period tended to see him as consumed by ambition for himself rather that Rome, but some later historians have been less sure. The fact is that Roman society had major problems for which the optimates had no real solutions, while Caesar was willing to try experiments like major public works and mandating that employers hire a certain number of free rather than slave laborers.

In terms of his ambition, Caesar was a product of his class and time. The contest for prestige and honor, for the consulship and other offices that made up the *cursus honorum*, was part of the fabric of everyday life for Rome's most distinguished families. Plutarch's history of Julius Caesar includes an anecdote that sums up not just Caesar's attitude, but those of his rivals. On his way to Gaul, Caesar and some of his officers stopped for the night in a tumbledown village. Would there be anyone in such a remote and poverty-stricken place, Caesar's companions wondered idly, who would want to be known as the first – the most important – man in this village? "Better the first man here than the second man in Rome," Caesar was said to have replied.

That trip to Gaul was itself an example of his ambition. Given the necessity for military renown to build a political career, Caesar took part in – and to a large extent started – a series of major wars with the Gallic tribes, built the first recorded bridge across the Rhine to invade Germany, and even invaded England, a land so remote many Romans thought it legendary. Caesar's own estimate was that a million Gauls and Germans died in those wars, and another million ended up enslaved. Even if these numbers are unrealistic, the wars had a catastrophic effect on these tribes, who at the time did not pose much of a military threat to Rome. Caesar's opponents pointed out that Roman traders were already a fixture in most of these areas before the Gallic Wars, and the wars produced little – furs, gold, even slaves – that could not have been gotten more cheaply and with less loss of life by trade.

Caesar was a man of manifold talents. Even Cicero, the most famous writer/orator of his day, said that if Caesar had dedicated his life to literature he would have gone down as one of the greatest writers of the Republic. His ability to act quickly and decisively in military matters was unmatched. On a personal level, the historian Suetonius, writing in the first century CE, said, "His friends he treated with invariable kindness and consideration," while "he never formed such bitter enmities that he was not glad to lay them aside when opportunity offered."

Given the sensitivity of his political antennae, it is hard to see how Caesar misread the level of unease that was created by his apparent willingness to accept the honors and trappings of kingship. Plutarch said of Republican Rome, "They suffered all things subjects should do by commandment of their kings; and yet they could not abide the name of a king, detesting it as the utter destruction of their liberty."

The lesson of Caesar's death was not lost on his successor. Octavian went on to rule Rome with a concentration of power Julius Caesar probably never imagined, but he concealed that power under the trappings and appearances of Republican institutions. Octavian and his successors, the great English historian of Rome Edward Gibbon remarked, constructed "an absolute monarchy disguised by the forms of a commonwealth." In Gibbon's words, they "surrounded their throne with darkness, concealed their irresistible strength, and humbly professed themselves the accountable ministers of the senate," the decrees of which they first dictated, and only then obeyed.

For Further Viewing

There are a number of worthwhile films of Shakespeare's *Julius Caesar*. The 1953 version directed by Joseph L. Mankiewicz boasts stars like Marlon Brando, James Mason, John Gielgud, Edmond O'Brien, Greer Garson, and Deborah Kerr. Though Brando clearly has little training in Shakespeare's language, his performance is memorable, and he was nominated for an Academy Award for best actor.

John Gielgud, who played Cassius in that 1953 version, played Caesar in the 1970 version, which starred Charlton Heston as Antony. (It was Heston's second

Antony – the first had been in a 1950 film.) The 1970 film was marred by a horribly misconceived performance by Jason Robards as Brutus, essentially the play's lead role. Robards, a fine American actor, employed what appeared to be a Method-style performance completely unsuitable to the text.

The BBC 1979 television version stars Richard Pasco as Brutus.

For a very watchable non-Shakespearean version of the Julius Caesar story, there is the 2006 HBO series, *Rome*. Ciarán Hinds plays Caesar in a fictionalized account that manages to illuminate both Caesar's character and the tangled politics of the late Roman Republic. James Purefoy is Marc Antony and Tobias Menzies plays Brutus.

2

"Her infinite variety"

Antony and Cleopatra

Julius Caesar and *Antony and Cleopatra* are Shakespeare's dramatizations of important elements in the history of the late Roman republic – the death of Julius Caesar and the struggle between Caesarian and Republican forces. *Julius Caesar* leads the audience through the story of Caesar's assassination and the defeat of the conspirators who killed him. *Antony and Cleopatra* takes the story further, describing the divisions among Caesar's loyalists after the conspirators have been defeated, and the eventual triumph of Caesar's heir Octavian – later the Emperor Augustus.

Both plays are based on history. But while *Julius Caesar* is a story that revolves around the relationship between ambition and ego, *Antony and Cleopatra* adds to that volatile mixture the relationship between ambition and love.

Background

Julius Caesar, the populist political–military leader, was assassinated in March of 44 BCE by senators who feared he was about to make himself king. His assassins were led by Brutus and Cassius. After Marc Antony's funeral oration for Caesar some days later, popular resentment at his murder drove Brutus, Cassius, and their allies from Rome.

Caesar's death came after a series of civil wars, from which he had emerged victorious. On his death the fault lines in Roman politics sprang open again. With Caesar's assassins fleeing to Asia, Caesar's surviving allies and adherents struggled with the Senate's aristocratic faction for control of Rome. One of those Caesarians was the young Octavian, Caesar's great-nephew, whose name (he called himself Julius Caesar) and status as Caesar's designated heir was enough to bring him substantial public and military support.

Octavian and Caesar's former deputy Marc Antony were technically allies. But both aspired to represent Caesar's legacy and to inherit his leadership. They managed to patch up their differences and, in cooperation with another military leader named Lepidus, formed a compact known as the Second Triumvirate (the First Triumvirate had been Julius Caesar, Crassus, and Pompey some years before) that effectively seized power.

The Second Triumvirate strengthened its hold on Rome by murdering hundreds of its opponents, including, as noted, the famous Roman writer/orator Cicero. The members then turned their attention to Caesar's assassins. Brutus and Cassius, who had killed Caesar in the name of the Republic, were using their offices in the rich provinces of the east to raise new armies to displace the triumvirate. Antony and Octavian raised their own troops, and in a series of battles (in which Antony was far more effective than the young and untrained Octavian) defeated the Republicans. Cassius and Brutus killed themselves, and the Republican cause was effectively lost.

Antony and Cleopatra picks up the story a few years later. The triumvirate has divided the Roman world among themselves, with Antony getting the rich and populous east, while Octavian got the west, including Italy, and Lepidus received Roman Africa.

Antony was by far the most senior and effective member of the trio, and many Romans expected him to emerge as the leading figure. (Plutarch says the young Octavian – sidelined by illness on important occasions – was in such bad shape after the final battle with the forces of Brutus and Cassius that he was not expected to survive for long.)

A Few Words About Antony

It may be generally true that history is written by the winners, but in Marc Antony's case the truth is more complicated. Among the principal surviving sources for the details of Marc Antony's life – for both Roman and modern historians – are the works of Cicero, who had a deep and profound dislike of Antony and who was murdered on Antony's orders. Cicero was one of the great writers of the Republic, and his works are still studied; as such, they have had a major effect on later historians and their views of Rome during this period. The memoirs of Octavian are also a source of our knowledge of Marc Antony. Whereas Octavian had little personal animus toward his onetime ally and later opponent, he was eager to justify his campaigns against the man who had been his adoptive father's trusted lieutenant, in addition to being Octavian's own colleague in the Second Triumvirate, as well as his brother-in-law. Under the circumstances, it would be understandable that Octavian's version of events would tend to magnify Antony's faults while minimizing his virtues.

Marc Antony was born in 83 or 82 BCE, to an aristocratic family. He had had something of a wild youth but later distinguished himself as a military man. Much of his career was spent serving with Caesar, and he was very popular with the troops. Caesar had left him in charge of Rome at one point, but Antony found peacetime service tedious. According to histories of this period, he had angered many upperclass (and other) Romans with his lack of attention to the everyday problems of running the city and had devoted his time to drinking bouts, banquets, theatrical displays, and other vulgar amusements, all in the company of lowborn types such as actors and dancers. According to Plutarch (a story he apparently got from Cicero's work), during this period Antony once appeared on official business in the Forum so drunk from the night before that he ended up vomiting into a cloak held by a friend. Such behavior by the man in authority was a major affront to Republican values.

Although the governing class of Rome was capable of endless disputes – even wars – over who had the authority to govern, this was true in part because they took governing very seriously. Military accomplishment was not enough. Candidates were also expected to display an interest in and capacity for administration.

Egypt and Cleopatra

Egypt was arguably Rome's most important client state. The annual flooding of the Nile made its banks the most productive agricultural region in the Mediterranean, and Rome depended on Egyptian grain to feed the city and the Italian peninsula. Egypt also had its own status in Roman eyes. Its civilization and its monuments were ancient – Egypt's beginnings were thousands of years older than Rome's own origins (and farther from Rome than Rome is from our civilization). Egypt's culture was cosmopolitan; its religion, with half-human, half-animal gods, was exotic. For its own internal political reasons Rome did not officially annex Egypt, largely because no one in power wanted to risk handing over its riches to an opposing faction of the Senate. But Roman military power made and unmade its monarchs.

Plutarch said of Cleopatra, "For her actual beauty, it is said, was not in itself so remarkable that none could be compared with her, or that no one could see her without being struck by it, but the contact of her presence, if you lived with her, was irresistible; the attraction of her person, joining with the charm of her conversation, and the character that attended all she said or did, was something bewitching. It was a pleasure merely to hear the sound of her voice, with which, like an instrument of many strings, she could pass from one language to another." Her dynasty was not originally Egyptian, but Greek, a relic of the empire of Alexander the Great. (The fact that she could speak Egyptian was thought remarkable.) She owed her throne specifically to Julius Caesar, who took her side in a dynastic dispute with her brother. Cleopatra's gratitude, along with her well-honed political skills, led to a political and personal relationship with Julius Caesar that yielded her son, Caesarion, whom Caesar never officially acknowledged. As noted in the previous chapter, she was in Rome when Caesar was assassinated, although she returned to Egypt following his death.

Her first meeting with Marc Antony may have been around 56 BCE, when she was a teenager and he was a staff officer serving in Egypt. We can presume they had some knowledge of each other when she was Caesar's mistress and he one of Caesar's key deputies. But their first recorded meeting post Caesar's death and the defeat of his assassins occurred when Antony, in his capacity as ruler of the Roman east, summoned Cleopatra to Tarsus to discuss matters of state. By the time their conference was over, he was smitten.

Sextus Pompey

Another major character in the history of the period is Sextus Pompey, son of the Pompey who was Julius Caesar's colleague in the First Triumvirate and later became his adversary. After the senior Pompey – defeated by Caesar at the Battle of Pharsalus – was murdered in Egypt, his sons took up the fight, first in North Africa and later in Spain. It was to defeat Pompey's sons that Julius Caesar went to Spain, and it was on his return from Spain that Shakespeare's *Julius Caesar* begins. Caesar's campaign had been successful, but one of Pompey's sons – Sextus Pompey – survived. In the confused political and military situation after Caesar's assassination, Sextus emerged as an important power, with his own legions and a very effective navy.

Parthian Shots

The play all but ignores Antony's campaign in Parthia, the site of incidents that historians view as key to his character. The Parthians, who occupied roughly what was later known as Persia, had humiliated Roman armies in 53 BCE with the routing of an expedition led by Crassus, a member of the First Triumvirate. To restore Roman honor, Julius Caesar had planned to wage a major campaign in Parthia – a plan prevented by his assassination. In 36 BCE, Antony, emboldened by the earlier success of his lieutenant Ventidius, embraced the challenge that Caesar had not lived to take up. Antony's initiative – operating far from his bases of support against well-trained and well-led forces on their home ground – did not go well. But Antony's failures on offense were atoned for by his management of his legions' strategic retreat under all but constant assault. Sharing his soldiers' meager rations and exposing himself to their dangers, he kept the army together as a fighting force in a nightmarish weeks-long trek until they reached friendly territory.

Chronology

In this play, as in the other histories, Shakespeare rearranges events and telescopes the timeline to suit his dramatic purposes. In brief, the real chronology of both plays is as follows:

44 BCE Julius Caesar assassinated

43 BCE Antony, Octavian, and Lepidus form a triumvirate to govern Rome

42 BCE The Caesarians, led principally by Marc Antony, defeat Brutus, Cassius and the Republican forces

41 BCE Cleopatra arrives in Greece to see Antony, now ruler of the east; Antony goes to Egypt

40 BCE Antony's wife Fulvia dies; he marries Octavia, sister of Octavian

37 BCE Triumvirs renew their pact, make alliance with Sextus Pompey

36 BCE Antony invades Parthia, manages fighting retreat, marries Cleopatra

34 BCE Antony announces that he is giving his children by Cleopatra the kingdoms of the east

32 BCE Antony's will is made public in Rome, including his desire to be buried in Egypt; Octavian and the Senate declare war (on Cleopatra)

31 BCE Battle of Actium between the combined forces of Antony and Cleopatra and those of Octavian; Octavian triumphs

30 BCE Battles at Alexandria; suicides of Antony and Cleopatra; Octavian eventually emerges as sole power in Rome

Act 1

The first scenes of the play establish for the audience Antony's neglect of his duties. In Egypt, two Roman friends of Antony decry the effects of his relationship with Cleopatra, saying that he, "triple pillar of the world" as one of the triumvirate, had become a "strumpet's fool." Proving them right, Antony refuses to hear a messenger from Rome with news from Octavian and Fulvia, Antony's wife (who had been challenging Octavian's power in Italy on Antony's behalf). Still, Antony finds time out of earshot of Cleopatra to hear the news of Fulvia's campaign against Octavian, and also learns that an army of Parthians is marching on Rome's eastern provinces – all while he lounges in Alexandria. Another messenger brings news of Fulvia's death (of natural causes).

"I must from this enchanting queen break off," mutters Antony, and in a speech to one of his aides details the declining political situation in Rome, particularly the rising power of Sextus Pompey, now master of much of the Mediterranean.

A scene between Octavian (called Caesar in the play and in real life) and Lepidus reprises for the audience the Roman opinion of Antony's dalliance that has come down to us, thanks in no small part to Octavian's propaganda campaign. They criticize the "lascivious wassails" that keep Antony from helping to deal with the threat Sextus Pompey poses to the triumvirate.

Act 2

Sextus Pompey, in a discussion with his officers, outlines the tensions among the triumvirs, and is surprised to learn that Antony has left Egypt for Rome. He had hoped that Cleopatra would "tie up the libertine in a field of feasts," thus keeping the ablest general, whose "soldiership is twice" that of Octavian and Lepidus, out of the struggle for power.

Antony may have cut short his Egyptian vacation, but his relationship with his fellow members of the triumvirate is still far from smooth. Octavian lays out his grievances, primarily that Antony's dead wife Fulvia went to war against him, that Antony ignored an agreement to provide Octavian with troops and aid, and that Antony had publicly ridiculed Octavian's messengers and dismissed them without a hearing.

To the first, Antony says that Fulvia was acting on her own, in part to create a conflict that would bring him back from Egypt (and presumably Cleopatra). To the second, he admits to having neglected, rather than having denied, his obligation; and to the third, he pleads to an excess of partying when Octavian's messenger had come to him: "Three kings I had newly feasted, and did want of what I was."

Antony's apology seems to have cooled the rancor of the conversation when Octavian's deputy Agrippa raises the possibility of Antony's remarriage, specifically to Octavia, Octavian's sister. Octavian objects, given Antony's relationship with Cleopatra, but Antony is interested. "I am not married, Caesar; let me hear Agrippa further speak." It requires only a few dozen lines before the business is concluded, and the bargain struck.

Alexandrian Luxury

Caesar's aide Maecenas asks about a report of their life in Alexandria. "Eight wild boars roasted whole for breakfast, and but twelve persons there. Is this true?" (The story is lifted directly from Plutarch, passed down to him from an acquaintance of one of his forbears.) Shakespeare's audience – there were wild boar in England then – would have known that one boar would have been more than enough, but Antony's aide Enobarbus makes light of the incident, saying, "[W]e had much more monstrous manner of feast" on other occasions.

Enobarbus's next speech gives Shakespeare the opportunity to make poetry out of Plutarch's description of Cleopatra's arrival in Greece to answer Antony's summons. Plutarch reports that royal barge arrived "with gilded stern and outspread sails of purple, while oars of silver beat time to the music of flutes and fifes and harps." But in Shakespeare's description it becomes

> The barge she sat in, like a
> burnished throne, burned on the water. The poop was
> beaten gold; purple the sails, and so perfumed that the
> winds were lovesick with them. The oars were silver,
> which to the tune of flutes kept stroke . . .

while Cleopatra herself "beggared all description."

It is in this conversation that Enobarbus dismisses the possibility that Antony would turn his back on Cleopatra in favor of Octavia. Enobarbus says of Cleopatra, "[A]ge cannot wither her, nor custom stale her infinite variety." His statement is borne out in the next scene. Taking his leave of Octavia, Antony acknowledges his wastrel reputation and uses a carpenter's metaphor to promise his new wife that he will do better: "I have not kept my square, but that to come shall all be done by the rule." However, before the scene is over he is making plans to return to Egypt, saying, "though I make this marriage for my peace, in the East my pleasure lies."

Shakespeare next dramatizes the meeting that led to a nonaggression pact between Sextus Pompey and the triumvirs, and follows it by a drinking bout that no doubt delighted Elizabethan audiences. The story comes from Plutarch. During the party, an aide to Sextus Pompey draws his leader aside to ask him if he would like to be the sole ruler of the Roman world. "These three world-sharers, these competitors, are in your vessel," says the aide. "Let me cut the cable; and when we are put off, fall to their throats." Pompey is clearly tempted but demurs, saying, "[T]his thou should'st have done, and not have spoken on it. . . . Being done unknown, I should have found it afterwards well done, but must condemn it now."

In a previous scene, Cleopatra vented her rage on a messenger who brought her the news of Antony's marriage. In the next, she demands of the same messenger a description of Octavia and decides that her rival is "dull of tongue and dwarfish." (Historians say Octavia was renowned for both her beauty and her temperament.)

The following scenes move rapidly between the west and the east and are designed to bring the audience up to speed with the historical story. While they are marked as separate scenes in modern editions, there were no scene breaks as such in the Elizabethan theater, and they probably would have been continuous, perhaps with the focus moving back and forth from one side of the stage to the other.

Lepidus Is Dismissed

The third of the triumvirs, Lepidus, distinguished himself in the previous drinking party by being the first to succumb, and was carried off. That scene's comedy becomes a metaphor in scene 5, as Enobarbus and Eros discuss Caesar's (offstage) dismissal of Lepidus from the triumvirs, supposedly for favoring Sextus Pompey in the wars that followed the breakdown of their treaty.

The next scene frames the major conflict of the play in Octavian's terms. Antony has appeared in public in Alexandria and divided the eastern empire into portions for his children by Cleopatra, all without consulting his colleague or the Senate. Octavia arrives in Rome not with honors due her station but "come like a market maid" to plead for her husband's cause, unaware that he has left their last home in Athens to return to Egypt. "Cleopatra hath nodded him to her. He hath given his empire up to a whore," says Octavian, who claims that Marc Antony and Cleopatra together are "levying the kings of the earth" to join them in war on Rome.

Although Shakespeare has compressed the action, the estrangement was a fact. Antony married Cleopatra under Egyptian law in 36 BCE. That marriage had no standing under Roman law, and he was officially married to Octavia until he divorced her in 32 BCE.

Octavian and his allies led a propaganda campaign against Antony, fueled by his unilateral granting of the eastern kingdoms to Cleopatra's children, his adoption of eastern manners of dress and behavior, and his treatment of Octavia, shabby even by the lax standards of the Roman aristocracy. Perhaps the final straw was his will, which was seized by Octavian from the Vestal Virgins and made public, showing that Antony had all but turned his back on Rome by wanting to be buried in Alexandria. The Senate then declared war on Cleopatra (not Antony) in 32 BCE.

Act 3

The Battle of Actium, which occupies much of act 3, occurred off the coast of Greece in 31 BCE. Some of Antony's allies believed his best chance for success was to invade Italy, where he still had many supporters and where, if he won, he could consolidate his power by taking Rome, a strategy that had worked for Julius Caesar. The problem was that Romans who had not taken sides in the conflict would not remain neutral if Antony arrived at the head of a force of Egyptians and other foreigners, turning what had been a civil war into a foreign invasion.

The discussion about whether to make the fight a sea battle or a land battle follows Plutarch closely. Also following Plutarch, Shakespeare treats the naval battle as having been lost when Antony, noticing Cleopatra's ships in flight and blinded by love, turned and followed them, abandoning the fight. However, there is another historical interpretation of these events. Under that theory, Antony realized that his land forces were surrounded and isolated by Octavian's. Antony also feared the power of Octavian's name and its resonance with the army. Rather than be starved out or see his legions desert to Octavian, Antony decided to stage a sea battle. It was his plan that when Octavian's force was occupied, he and Cleopatra would make a run for Egypt with the heart of his navy, along with the treasure ships that held the funds he needed to keep the war going.

Whether Antony's flight was panic or stratgem, the Battle of Actium was won by Octavian. Most of Antony's land forces, which had watched the sea battle from the shoreline and never engaged, eventually ended up laying down their arms on Octavian's promise of fair treatment.

Shakespeare follows Plutarch closely in his account of Antony's mood after the loss at Actium. Although in the play Shakespeare does not go into it, Plutarch says that when Antony eventually made his way to Alexandria, he had a house built on a spit of land in the harbor and lived alone, emulating the legendary misogynist Timon of Athens (subject of other plays, including one by Shakespeare). Eventually, Antony returned to Cleopatra and they reassumed their roistering ways.

Some months later, Octavian's forces arrived off Alexandria to finally resolve the issue. In one early battle, Antony defeated them soundly, but in a subsequent naval engagement his troops – realizing the fears he had at Actium – went over to Caesar's side without a fight. Antony then understood that all was lost, and Shakespeare's version follows Plutarch's account of him stabbing himself, being taken to Cleopatra's tomb, being lifted up by Cleopatra and her maids, and dying.

Cleopatra's Death

When he entered Alexandria, Octavian did not take Cleopatra into custody, though he did leave her under guard. She killed herself when she became convinced that Octavian was unwilling to leave her on her throne and wanted her alive only for her value in his triumphal parade. According to Plutarch, she had made a careful study of the effects of various poisons by applying them to condemned criminals, and decided on the bite of an asp as the least disfiguring and painful.

The extent of Octavian's desire to keep her alive is open to question. If he had been truly interested in doing so he could have secured her elsewhere, rather than leaving her in her own mausoleum. But there is no question that he hoped to preserve the treasures she had piled up in her tomb because he desperately needed Egyptian funds to pay off his debts, particularly to the legions (including Antony's, who had surrendered on his promise of pay). He granted her last request that she be buried beside Antony.

She had sent her son Caesarion, now a young man, to the east to get him out of harm's way. He was lured back to Egypt on a pretense, where Octavian, unwilling to tolerate another claimant to Caesar's patrimony, had him strangled. Antony's oldest son by Fulvia was also executed, on the excuse that he had taken part in the resistance. Antony and Cleopatra's other children were eventually taken back to Rome to march in Octavian's triumph. According to the historian Dio Cassius, an image of their mother dead on a couch was part of the procession. Octavian's parade occupied three days, celebrating victories over some northern tribes, the naval battle at Actium, and the subjugation of Egypt. Said Plutarch: "Now all the processions proved notable, thanks to the spoils from Egypt – in such quantities, indeed had spoils been gathered there that they sufficed for all the processions – but the Egyptian celebration surpassed them all for costliness and magnificence."

After the triumph, Cleopatra's children were reared in Rome by Antony's widow Octavia, along with her children by Antony and his surviving children by Fulvia. When they were of age, Cleopatra's children were placed in favorable marriages in Roman client states. Octavian consolidated his power, took the name Augustus in 28 BCE, and ruled until 14 CE.

Historians often date his reign from his victory at the
Battle of Actium.

Love and Ambition

It was the nearly universal attitude of Roman writers
that Antony had been turned from his duty and
blinded by love. Cleopatra's motivation was more
a matter of conjecture. Was she acting as a woman
driven by love or as a monarch driven by ambition?
The question reflects the complicated role of women
in Roman society. Roman women, though technically
completely subject to their husbands, possessed
substantial influence. Many upperclass Roman women
were key advisers of their husbands and sons in matters
of government and politics. ("We rule the world, but
our wives rule us," no less an authority than Cicero
remarked.) But it was one thing to rely in private on
one's wife, quite another to be seen to do so, or for
that matter to allow one's affection – even for a spouse
– to divert one from the business of government.

A strongly antimonarchical sentiment also pre-
occupied much of Roman politics. Julius Caesar had been
assassinated in part because he refused to recognize the
strength of this emotion. While many knowledgeable
observers saw Antony as potentially less of a threat
to the Republic than Octavian, the fact that Antony
was tied to a foreign monarch did his Republican
reputation no good. Significant numbers of Romans
were also profoundly disturbed at the thought that
their most distinguished military leader was shirking
his duties in managing half the Empire to wallow in
luxury and base amusements in a competing capital.

(Meanwhile, Octavian was cultivating a public lifestyle of modesty and respectability.)

Roman xenophobia also concealed a certain amount of unstated fear. By this time, Rome was clearly the political and military center of the Mediterranean – indeed, the center of the western European world. But Athens remained the intellectual and aesthetic center, and the Greek east in general was by far the richest, the most civilized, and most productive part of the empire. Most educated Romans spoke Greek in addition to Latin, had Greek tutors for their children, and were entertained by arts that emulated Greek forms.

Many Romans had a secret fear that the center of the empire could be moved to the Greek east; worries that were amplified by the thought that Julius Caesar, if named a king outside Italy, might find it useful to locate his court and capital where he was so acknowledged. Antony's desire to be buried in Alexandria confirmed this fear in many hearts. Whatever the reality of that possibility at the time of these events, this in fact did eventually come to pass. The Emperor Constantine created a "New Rome" at Constantinople in 330 CE and moved his capital there. It was a stroke from which the "old" Rome never recovered.

For Further Viewing

Jonathan Miller directed the 1981 BBC television version of *Antony & Cleopatra*, with Colin Blakely as Antony and Jane Lapotaire as Cleopatra. Charlton

Heston directed himself as Marc Antony in the 1972 film, with Hildegarde Neil as Cleopatra. Timothy Dalton and Lynn Redgrave starred in a 1983 television version.

The most remarkable non-Shakespearean version of the story is undoubtedly the 1963 film *Cleopatra* starring Elizabeth Taylor, with Richard Burton as Marc Antony and Rex Harrison as Julius Caesar. An epic in every sense and the most expensive picture of its time, it did not fare well with many critics, and some audiences were put off by its four-hour length. Director Joseph L. Mankiewicz reportedly wanted to release it as two movies, each three hours in length – one centering on Cleopatra and Caesar, the other on Cleopatra and Marc Antony – but the studio balked. The movie is also notable for its credits, which include the historians Plutarch, Suetonius, and Appian, whose works the screenwriters consulted in creating the story.

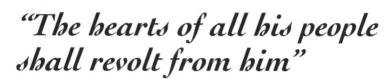

3

"The hearts of all his people shall revolt from him"

King John

The event that led to the conflict in this play – and the ensuing decades of conflict between the English and the French – happened more than a hundred years earlier.

For centuries England had been part of the German/Scandinavian world. Its name and the language its inhabitants spoke were derived from North German invaders – the Angles. Centuries later it was subjected to Viking raids, and so pervasive was the Viking influence that much of eastern England was officially the Danelaw – an area where Danish rather than English law prevailed. When King Edward the Confessor died in the eleventh century, the king of Norway claimed the English throne. He was opposed by Harold Godwinson, who had more native roots, and the two sides fought it out in a battle between Norse invaders and the English in northeast England, at Stamford Bridge. Godwinson and the

English won but immediately had to turn around and head south. Soon after they arrived – depleted and exhausted – they were involved in another battle, this one against forces led by William the Bastard (the appellation refers to his parentage rather than his character) of Normandy, who had ties of his own to the English crown. The battle was at Hastings, the year was 1066 CE, and Godwinson's defeat turned William the Bastard into William the Conqueror. It also moved England decisively into the orbit of France and Continental Europe, eventually creating a set of political and property entanglements that would lead to centuries of on-and-off warfare.

The Angevins

A century after William's triumph, the crown passed to Henry II of England, King John's father. He had inherited not just England, but vast territories in France, from Normandy in the north through central France; then through his wife, the remarkable Eleanor of Aquitaine, he had also gained control of a huge swath of southern France. In fact, Henry controlled much more of France than did the French king, whose territories consisted largely of the area around Paris.

Other parts of France were run by more or less independent nobles. They were technically vassals of the French king, as was Henry for his French possessions, even though he was a king in his own right in England. But the exact duties incumbent upon such relationships were subject to many interpretations. As W. L. Warren, a biographer of John, noted of French nobles of the period in his book *King John*, "[T]hey were loyal to their duke in that they would turn out to fight for him against anyone else, but they expected to be left alone in their counties." It was not unusual for a lord to lead a military expedition against one of his vassals to enforce his will.

Such expeditions were only part of the hands-on nature of medieval kingship. To maintain their control in an era when communication was difficult and there were few of the bureaucratic institutions that help government function, kings traveled constantly. The Angevins – Henry II and his sons, Richard (the Lion-Hearted) and John – were no exceptions, and with an empire that stretched from northern England to southern France, they had a great deal of ground to cover.

Although the Angevins (named for the French district of Anjou) may have been kings of England, that did not make them English. Their native language was French, and their principal possessions were on the Continent. Henry II divided his time among all his possessions; Richard, brought up in southern France and serving all across the dominions and in the Middle East, spent relatively little time in England, even while he reigned. John himself was as likely to be in France as he was in England at any given time during his kingship.

A Delicate Balance

In societies like those of the European Middle Ages, it was good to be the king, but not necessarily great.

No king could expect a successful reign without the support of a significant number of nobles, who generally had independent military power through the knights who owed them allegiance. A king could afford to anger a certain number of nobles, but when he lost the support of a majority or of the most powerful families, he could face rebellion.

The concept of absolute monarchy was not widespread in medieval Europe, and inheritance of the crown was far from a standardized process. The oldest surviving son of a deceased king clearly had a significant claim on the crown, but there were often other circumstances that had to be taken into account. The king was first and last a war leader of his people, so a son unavailable for such efforts because of age or inclination would generally not earn the approval of key nobles. In office, the king had to balance his alliances carefully among the important nobles to keep a working majority of support, or at least to prevent a significant number of nobles from becoming so unhappy they would look for a replacement. In addition, the royal household was the financial responsibility not of the nation (there really wasn't a modern concept of nation) but of the king's family estates, and an ambitious king with a large realm was under constant money pressure.

The Crusades

The peripatetic nature of medieval kingship in Europe was made even more complicated by side trips to the Middle East in the form of the Crusades. This extension of Europe's power into new or former territories was the fruit of a papal strategy to kill two birds with one stone – to channel the destructive violence of Europe's warrior class and to heal a breach between the eastern and western branches of Christendom.

One of the biggest complaints of medieval society was the level of violence perpetrated by the nobles, who all but monopolized military power; they often ruled their estates with no regard for justice (they were the judges in local courts) and their knights and men-at-arms terrorized local populations when they weren't attacking each other at local tournaments. Far from the familiar image of noble knights jousting with lances, these contests were free-for-all melees designed to capture horses, weapons, and even knights for sale or ransom. The destruction of crops and villages, and the more-than-occasional deaths of participants and bystanders, were regarded as acceptable collateral damage.

In 1095 CE, after requests from the Byzantine emperor, Pope Urban II preached a crusade to recover Jerusalem and other holy places, which had been in Muslim hands for several centuries. The appeal touched a nerve in the profoundly religious society of eleventh century Europe. Although it had been assumed that military men (and nobles were first and last military men) would answer the call, thousands of civilians also volunteered.

Few occasions better illustrate the law of unintended consequences than the First Crusade. Civilian mobs began their journey by massacring the Jewish communities in the Rhine Valley and alienated the Byzantines when they finally made their way to

Constantinople. The civilian Crusaders were then (to the relief of the Byzantines) slaughtered by the Turks when they attempted to bring them to battle. The military arm of the First Crusade was somewhat more successful, taking the city of Acre in Asia Minor (but refusing to give it up to the Byzantine Emperor) before moving on and conquering Jerusalem. Their victory was somewhat marred by their immediate and indiscriminate massacre of the city's inhabitants, Muslim, Jew, and Christian alike.

By the time of the play there had been several more Crusades with varying degrees of success, and some of the major figures mentioned in the play – particularly John's brother, Richard the Lion-Hearted – had taken part. Getting King John to go on crusade was one of the goals of the papacy, a fact that (as we shall see in the play) John used as leverage to help him deal with his political problems at home and abroad.

The Crusades backfired on the Byzantine emperors, who found themselves not with a new ally in the region but a new competitor. In 1204, a Crusader fleet and army, under the influence of Venice, sacked Constantinople and installed a new emperor.

The Issues at Hand

The background for all the action in the play is the desire of King John to hold on to the extensive Angevin dominions in France, while Philip, king of France, and his son, Louis the Dauphin, seek to expand theirs, largely at John's expense. Their principal strategy is to push forward a rival candidate for the English crown,

John's nephew Arthur, son of his older brother. While Arthur's fate is central to the drama, Arthur himself is only a chess piece in the French king's game. Meanwhile, John's heavy exactions of money and military resources are the real reason for the unhappiness of many of his English barons, who were, at best, unenthusiastic about much of the fighting in France. While the nobles understood the importance of fighting for Normandy, where many had lands and relatives, they had less interest in central and southern France. These areas were John's possessions through his wife and through inheritance, and were not traditionally Norman or English.

Act 1

The play opens with a confrontation between King John and a French envoy, who demands in the name of the French king that John lay aside his crown in England and France in favor of his nephew Arthur. What should result from John's refusal? "Bloody war," says the Frenchman. "War for war and blood for blood," John responds, sending the envoy on his way with the warning that John's troops will follow closely (in fact, John and the Angevin kings had a deserved reputation for speedy military maneuvers, a telling advantage in most wars, particularly medieval ones).

The story of the patrimony of Faulconbridge is not in traditional English accounts, but the chronicler Edward Hall tells a similar story of a young Frenchman known as the Bastard of Orleans, who embraced an illegitimate tie to the house of Orleans rather than his father's estate. This, somewhat altered, may have been Shakespeare's source. Whatever its origin, it serves to highlight an oft-neglected side of King John – his interest in the law and his significant activity as a judge in legal matters large and small. Although John has gone down in much of history as lazy, unprincipled, and untrustworthy, according to some sources he was much in demand by plaintiffs of all estates – particularly common appellants – to preside in lawsuits.

The particular case in question – which of the sons of Faulconbridge should inherit – might well have been a royal question in any case. Under feudal law, John as king was in some sense the owner of such estates. When a noble died, his heir would be forced to pay the king a fee in order to get his inheritance, and if there were no immediate heir the estate would in effect become the king's until an heir was determined.

Act 2

The opening scene of act 2 is full of ahistorical elements. The king of France introduces the duke of Austria to Arthur as the man who killed Richard the Lion-Hearted, "the forerunner of thy blood." Richard was Arthur's uncle, not his father; the duke was actually not the man in question, because Richard had died in a siege at the hands of a similarly named noble; when King Philip announces that "our cannon shall be bent against the brows of this resisting town," he was anticipating technological advances in warfare, for cannons did not come into use in Europe until a century or more after the events of this play.

The confrontation between King John's mother, Queen Eleanor, and Arthur's mother, Constance, is one of the great scenes of its kind in Shakespeare. Says the Holinshed chronicles, "Surely the king's mother Eleanor was sore against her nephew (actually her grandson) Arthur, rather moved thereto by envy conceived against his mother." Shakespeare sums it up more neatly in Queen Eleanor's words to Constance: "Thy bastard shall be a king that thou mayst be queen."

The story of the siege of Angiers, the ancestral seat of the Angevin dynasty, is relatively straightforward in the play, but a good deal more complicated in the sources. Holinshed says that at one point Queen Eleanor and John's mercenary forces took the town, which had declared for Arthur, "slew many of the citizens and committed the rest to prison." Apparently resistance was not quashed, because Holinshed goes on to talk about John encircling the town, breaking through the gates, and delivering it to his soldiers as a prize, "So that, of the citizens, some were taken, some killed, and the walls of the city beaten flat to the ground."

In the play, the political marriage of John's niece, Blanche, and Louis, heir to the French throne, for the moment quashes the coming war. In reality, it did reduce tensions between England and France; afterward Arthur paid homage to the French king for the possessions in Brittany and other districts in France that had come to Arthur from his father, Geoffrey, King John's older brother. According to

Holinshed, despite the apparent rapprochement, Arthur then remained with the French rather than go with his uncle John, "who (as he supposed) did bear him little good will."

Act 3

Even as Constance is baiting King Philip and the duke of Austria for making a deal with John and abandoning her son's cause ("This day of shame, oppression, perjury. . . ."), Shakespeare has a legate from the pope, Cardinal Pandulph, appear on the scene to complicate John's life and undermine his new alliance with France. The issue in question was the appointment of the new Archbishop of Canterbury. John had a candidate for this prominent church post, but the pope had his own, Stephen Langton. (Such conflicts between the papacy and royal figures across Europe were relatively common.) Langton was an Englishman but had spent most of his church life in Paris, and John was convinced he was sympathetic to John's enemies. The conflict led first to a papal interdict, which banned the clergy from saying mass or administering the sacraments in England. John, ever short of money, used the occasion to collect the revenues from English parishes, with the logic that since the clergy could not perform their functions, they deserved no salaries. Realizing the failure of this tactic, Pope Innocent III eventually excommunicated John and urged all Christian princes to take arms against him.

John's proud rejoinder in the play, that "no Italian priest shall tithe or toll in our dominions" without his permission, is a statement that would have had great resonance for Shakespeare's audience. Despite many conflicts and much suspicion of the Catholic Church for its wealth and power, it was still a unifying influence in Western Europe in John's time. By Shakespeare's age, after the rise of Lutheranism, Henry VIII's break with Rome, and the attempted invasion of England by the Spanish Armada to restore Catholicism, there was little popular sentiment for the papacy, particularly in London where the plays were produced.

In the play, Pandulph's excommunication of John undoes the alliance with France and leads to a battle in which French forces are defeated and Arthur is captured. In Holinshed's history, the story again is rather different. In his account, Queen Eleanor was fortified in the French city of Mirabeau when it was captured by forces led by Arthur, who treated her "very honorably, and with great reverence," (though Holinshed quotes other sources who said she escaped capture only to barricade herself in a tower). In any case King John soon arrived, defeated Arthur's forces, rescued his mother, and captured Arthur. Arthur was unchastened by defeat and imprisonment ("abounding too much in his own willful opinion," says Holinshed). Rather than trying to come to some kind of settlement with his uncle, he instead demanded of John that he resign his crown and all his lands. John, being in Holinshed's phrase "sore moved" by his nephew's words, ordered him imprisoned, first at Falais and then Rouen.

In the play Pandulph and Arthur's mother Constance understand immediately the fate that awaits Arthur. So does the audience, as John takes aside Hubert, to whom he has given charge of Arthur's imprisonment, and says "cast an eye on yon young boy . . . he is a very serpent in my way." Though Hubert promises to "keep him so that he shall not offend thy majesty," John responds with a single word: "Death."

In another memorable scene, Constance appears, hair undone, mourning Arthur's coming death. She says, "Grief fills up the room of my absent child, lies in his bed, walks up and down with me. . . ." The constant references to her hair – "this hair I tear is mine" and King Philip's repeated "bind up those tresses" – had a significant meaning for Shakespeare's contemporaries. During this time, no respectable married woman would appear outside her home or even her bedroom with her hair undone or uncovered, and the gesture was meant to convey to the audience the depth of Constance's despair. Although the scene is powerful, it is a complete invention. Constance died of natural causes before Arthur was captured. Arthur, when he oversaw the siege of Mirabeau and was taken, was about sixteen. By medieval standards he was an adult of military age, rather than the boy Shakespeare portrays.

After the French defeat, Pandulph explains the political realities to Louis, who is mourning the loss of the battle to John. "'Tis strange to think how much King John hath lost in this which he accounts so clearly won," says Pandulph, who predicts that the capture of Arthur will lead to the loss of his throne.

"That John may stand, then Arthur needs must fall," Pandulph tells him. Then, at the news of Arthur's inevitable death, John's support will wither as "the hearts of all his people shall revolt from him."

Arthur's Death

In the play, Hubert arrives at Arthur's prison with the executioners and is dissuaded from putting out the boy's eyes by a heartfelt appeal from Arthur (who in many productions since Shakespeare's time has been played by a girl). According to another chronicler, Ralph of Coggeshall, the executioners' charge was to not only put out Arthur's eyes but to remove his genitals, making it impossible for him to accomplish the primary functions of a medieval monarch – to produce an heir as well as to lead his forces in war.

In Holinshed's account, Hubert, having stopped the execution, tried to reduce the unrest among Arthur's adherents by spreading a rumor that Arthur had died, and he went so far as to distribute Arthur's clothing to a leper hospital. The reaction among Arthur's sympathizers was so strong that Hubert later had to admit that Arthur was still alive. King John, says Holinshed, was not displeased that his order had been disobeyed, since his captains told him that "he should not find knights to keep his castles" if Arthur had been so tortured because the knights would fear the same treatment if they fell into their enemies' hands.

Arthur's actual death, according to Holinshed, might have happened as Shakespeare describes, in an accidental fall, or from disease. Some chroniclers record allegations that John strangled Arthur during a drunken rage. "Certain it is," Holinshed reports, that Arthur "was removed unto Rouen . . . out of which there was not any that would confess ever seeing him leave alive."

Reconciliation with Rome

John, surrounded by opponents domestic and foreign, eventually came to understand the necessity of reconciliation with the papacy. Shakespeare mentions, but chooses not to dramatize, the actual ceremony in which John handed over his crown to Cardinal Pandulph, who in the pope's name shortly returned it. This symbolic act to demonstrate John's fealty to Rome had little effect on the day-to-day governance of England. But it did swing the pope to John's side, and he brought his influence to bear in settling the war with France that the church had previously encouraged. Many barons, however, were enraged that John would take such a step, in part because it reduced their own status, making them the subjects of a vassal rather than subjects of a king.

As a result of the reconciliation with Rome, Pandulph went to France to try to dissuade King Philip from the war; although Philip heard him out, he "by no means would be turned from the execution of his purpose," says Holinshed. Meanwhile, the royal marriage John had agreed to in order to calm the waters between England and France (see act 2) backfired. Two important English nobles, the earl of Winchester and Robert Fitz Walter, came to France and offered the English crown to Louis, who as the new husband of John's niece Blanche was the senior male relative in the Angevin line (other than John himself). Thus emboldened, Louis invaded England with a significant force, and was embraced by "a great number of those lords and gentlemen which had sent for him . . . as if he had been their true and natural prince."

John was not easily cowed. He had further strengthened his ties to the papacy by declaring his intention to go on crusade, making him in effect immune from a number of medieval legal processes. Despite the divisions within the kingdom, he mounted a vigorous defense, his naval forces routing a French fleet twice its size, a "famous victory," in Holinshed's words, that Shakespeare does not cover. The struggle, in reality a civil war, was a back-and-forth-affair, with important nobles changing sides (the story of the English lords on Louis's side abandoning him upon learning of the French plan to have them executed comes straight from Holinshed).

The End of John

John's death came after a military reverse. At one point, his baggage train, with the supplies and money he needed to prosecute the war, was lost to a sudden flooding of the channel of a river. John was taken ill shortly thereafter. One explanation given by Holinshed blamed the king's "immoderate feeding on raw peaches, and drinking of new cider." He also gives an alternate explanation, that John was poisoned by a monk, the explanation adopted by Shakespeare. Prince Henry – whose presence at

his father's death is ahistorical, was named Henry III
at the age of nine. While the play credits Cardinal
Pandulph with persuading Louis to abandon the
campaign and return to France, it was actually
much later, after significant defeats, that Louis was
permitted to withdraw to France.

What Is Not in the Play: Magna Carta and the Crowning of Louis

To the extent that there is a popular perception of
King John, it is as the villainous prince of the Robin
Hood story; he is also sometimes remembered as the
king who was forced by his barons to sign Magna
Carta, often identified as the foundation of modern
democratic government. Yet, Shakespeare makes no
mention of it in the play.

Magna Carta has acquired a huge reputation, but
that reputation took centuries to grow. Signed by
John under pressure in 1215 CE at Runnymede,
its articles addressed a wide range of the barons'
immediate complaints. It covers the relationship
between the king and his nobles, and makes
little mention of the common people. Nor was it
particularly original – much of it is taken from a
previous Charter of Liberties granted by Henry I
nearly a century earlier.

While never completely forgotten, in the immediate
centuries afterward Magna Carta was regarded as
merely another milestone in the ongoing conflict
between the king and the semi-independent warlords
who made up the nobility.

It was not until after Shakespeare's time that Magna Carta was rediscovered as a potential weapon in the battle between the king and another group interested in limiting royal power – parliament. It was quoted often during the revolution of the seventeenth century that saw the execution of King Charles I. Its success as a legal precursor and propaganda weapon during that revolution led to its reuse for similar purposes by the American colonists, and it has since been enshrined as a fountainhead of the U.S. form of democratic government.

The Invasion

It was shortly after the barons forced John to sign Magna Carta in 1215 that the Dauphin of the play, Louis of France, arrived in England with a huge invasion force. He ended up in London (a center of anti-John sentiment) where he was crowned king of England before a crowd of supporting English nobles at St. Paul's. Given Shakespeare's audience and the anti-French sentiment of most of the history plays, it is hardly surprising that he chose to avoid this at best unflattering incident in the history of the English nation-state.

John's Character

John's real-life character has been the subject of much debate among students of English history. His nephew's mysterious death left something of a blot on his name, but he is not the only English monarch to have rivals to the throne disappear under mysterious circumstances. Given his struggles with the church, it is not surprising that contemporary chroniclers, most of whom were monks or otherwise tied to the church, saw him as profoundly flawed, if not actually evil. (In personal practice he was said, like Henry VIII, to have been conventionally devout.) Holinshed says of writers of the time, "scarcely can they afford him a good word." However, Tudor writers saw that conflict with the church through very different eyes, and John's virtues were rediscovered. But the enshrinement of Magna Carta as a foundation of modern democracy once again put John, who signed under protest and later sought to undermine the accord, in a bad light. Holinshed writes that John had "a princely heart," though "in his rage his immoderate displeasure" caused him to miss now and then "that which otherwise he might have brought to pass." The anonymous Barnwell chronicler, a contemporary, summed him up this way: "A great prince certainly," but "scarcely a happy one."

For Further Viewing

The reign of King John is not a story many dramatists have rushed to portray, but his parents have been the subject of several excellent dramas. His father's tumultuous relationship with Thomas à Becket was the source for T. S. Eliot's 1935 play, *Murder in the Cathedral*, and the 1964 film *Becket*. The relationship between Henry II and Queen Eleanor of Aquitaine (which had plenty of tumult of its own) was the subject of the play and 1968 film *The*

Lion in Winter. Peter O'Toole plays King Henry II in both films, opposite Richard Burton as Becket in the former and Katharine Hepburn as Eleanor of Aquitaine in the latter.

The 1984 BBC version of Shakespeare's *King John* is available on DVD. It features Leonard Rossiter as King John and a remarkable performance by Claire Bloom as Constance.

4

"What subject can give sentence on his King?"

Richard II

The first of the English history plays, *King John*, was set about 1215 CE and is something of an outlier in the cycle. *Richard II* is the true beginning of Shakespeare's connected stories of the rise and fall of a series of medieval English monarchs.

As noted, in 1215 CE England was one of the realms governed by the Angevins, a French-speaking dynasty with great landholdings not just in England, but also in the west and south of France. The story of King John was in large part that of the struggle between John and the kings of France – whose actual power was then confined to a small section around Paris – over who was to govern France.

By 1400 CE – roughly the year that Shakespeare sets the first in the cycle of plays that culminate with *Richard III* – that struggle was far from over, but the nations involved had changed a great deal. In King John's time, England had been just one of the territories of the French-speaking Angevin dynasty, and the ruling class was heavily French in language and outlook. By the reign of Richard II, English had become much more common among the upper classes, and Richard himself is one of the first monarchs whom we know to have been able to speak and read English fluently (in addition, of course, to French and Latin). But the issue of who would govern France was far from settled, although the Capetian dynasty, based in Paris, was expanding and extending its power.

The Hundred Years' War

The English and French royal families were very closely related, the result of diplomatic marriages and ancient family ties. In 1328, King Charles IV of France died with no direct male heir. Among the claimants to his throne was Charles's nephew, the English king Edward III, whose mother had been Charles's sister. Whether or not Edward III actually thought he could become king of France is a question debated by historians. Some believe that Edward's claim to the French throne was a bargaining chip he was prepared to abandon if he could get something else.

Two immediate issues were the French regions of Aquitaine and Gascony. Aquitaine was a part of southern France that had come into English hands with the marriage of King John's mother, Eleanor of Aquitaine, to John's father, but over the course of nearly two hundred years the French kings had whittled away at English sovereignty in the area. Gascony was a region in southwest France with strong commercial ties to England. A number of important Gascons saw an advantage in enduring the remote government of England rather than the control of a closer king based in Paris.

The major opening battle of Edward's campaign for the French crown was at the French town of Crecy in 1346 CE, where a smaller force of English infantry and longbowmen, using better equipment and tactics, all but annihilated the armored knights who constituted the flower of French chivalry. The battle was fought again some ten years later, with a similar victory at Poitiers. But Edward III was not able to translate these victories into the actual crown of France.

These battles constituted the opening salvos of the Hundred Years' War, which actually lasted well over a century, though it was intermittent. The expense of equipping, transporting, and maintaining in the field a major military force was more than late medieval governments could manage on a regular basis. Consequently, the war was marked by sharp engagements followed by years of relative peace, particularly in the decades after the bubonic plague struck Europe in the middle of the fourteenth century. The principal English war leader for much of this time was Edward III's son, Edward. Known as the Black Prince (from the color of his armor), his military skill made him one of the most admired figures of the period, including by some of his enemies. However, while he was on the Continent, Edward fell ill. He returned to England a semi-invalid, and died in 1376. A year later, the prince's father, King Edward III, died, and the crown passed to the Black Prince's ten-year-old son, who was crowned Richard II.

The Plague and England in 1400

When the Hundred Years' War began, the populations of England and France had grown substantially from the year 1200 (the period of *King John*), with a particular increase in the number and size of towns. But in 1346, bubonic plague, which had arrived in Genoa from the east, swept through Europe. It killed millions on the Continent, then struck England, where its effects were felt most heavily by the working classes in the crowded cities and towns, but also on the villages of the countryside. Perhaps as much as one-third of the English population died. Ironically, the surviving members of the laboring classes were economically better off once the plague had passed. Before the plague, England had become a place where there were more workers than work. After the plague, there was a shortage of workers, which allowed their wages to rise significantly and gave them a new sense of empowerment, as reflected in the popular uprisings known as the Peasants' and Jack Cade's rebellions (ignored by Shakespeare in this play but effectively combined in the *Henry VI* trilogy).

A Note on Names

One of the most confusing aspects of Shakespeare's history plays is the fact that important characters have a number of names and titles, which are used interchangeably. Many nobles used the place of their birth as their basic name. Thus, Richard II, born in France while his father was stationed there, was first known as Richard of Bourdeaux. His uncle John, who had been born in Ghent in the Low Countries, was known as John of Ghent (anglicized to Gaunt). As a brother of King Edward III, John was already a duke, but then he inherited through his first wife the Lancaster fortune and the title duke of Lancaster.

Another of Richard's uncles, Thomas of Woodstock, was also duke of Gloucester. Richard's principal antagonist in this play, Henry Bolingbroke (the name was drawn from where he was born), is also known as Henry of Hereford (from the title of an earldom he held). As the son of John of Gaunt on his father's death he became entitled to call himself the duke of Lancaster before he became King Henry IV. Then, as now, English noblemen also had subsidiary titles. Richard's friend, the duke of Aumerle, lost his ducal title after Richard was deposed but retained the title of earl of Rutland (and his father reminds his mother to refer to him so in act 5).

The History

From the beginning, Richard's was a troubled reign. Although there was no official regency, his uncles dominated the government during his teens. The one remarkable incident of his minority was the uprising in 1381 CE known as the Peasants' Rebellion. The revolt, which included not just peasants but also small landholders and artisans, was in response to repeated taxations. Thousands of people marched on London to see the youthful king and to ask – or demand – that he remove corrupt officials and roll back taxes. They murdered some officials along the way and burned some estates, including the London-area mansion of Richard's uncle, John of Gaunt.

With no standing army and no police force to speak of, the English government at the outset could barely resist. The young Richard, accompanied by a few officials, eventually met the protestors on a field outside the city. The situation, already risky, became dangerous when the rebels' leader, Wat Tyler, was killed in a scuffle with one of Richard's party. Richard saved the day by mounting a horse, announcing to the crowd that he was their new leader, and leading them away from the city. Believing his pledges to reform the administration, the crowd eventually dispersed. Richard fulfilled none of his promises, and the remaining leaders of the uprising were found and punished, some with execution. (An important event in the reign of Richard II, Shakespeare ignores the Peasants' Rebellion in this play, dramatizing it later by conflating it with a similar demonstration during the reign of Henry VI.)

As he grew older, Richard asserted himself as king, appointing his own officials and taking more of the reins of government into his own hands. Unfortunately, as he did so he managed to alienate more and more of his subjects, both members of the nation's elite landholding families and the parliamentary commons, a voice for the rural gentry and the growing urban commercial class.

The landholding families were offended by Richard's elevation of relative unknowns to important positions of power in the administration. This was more than mere jealousy. The king shared power with these elite families as a body, but he was more than first among equals. He could assign vacant estates or revenues from various enterprises, such as port duties, to them. The king's preferment brought not just prestige, but wealth. The elite families, accustomed to dividing these resources among themselves, were alarmed to see people they regarded as outsiders replacing them. The parliamentary commons were also alarmed, in their case at the increasing burden of taxation. Unlike the modern governments of industrial nations, countries at this time had very few resources. The king was expected to support the royal household out of his own estates, whereas duties on imports and exports carried most of the burden of financing what was left of the national administration.

Wars were undertakings of extraordinary expense. Typically, the king would have to ask parliament to raise a one-time tax to mount and sustain an expedition. Parliament did so out of a mixture of national pride and the expectation of commercial gain. Such benefits might include the capture of coastal cities where the English could trade or concessions in manufacturing towns like the clothing production centers in the Low Countries, which were generally subject to France and were a critical link in the largest export industry

England had, the wool trade. Richard, however, had a profound distaste for wars with the French, and his reign was marked by a long pause in the hostilities of the Hundred Years' War. Nevertheless, the burdens of taxation did not diminish, in part because of his increasingly extravagant court and lifestyle.

In 1387–88, the general unhappiness with Richard's administration resulted in what amounted to a coup d'etat by a group of important nobles known as the Lords Appellant, who accused Richard's closest advisers of misgovernment. Although the accounts vary, one school of historians believes that Richard, who had taken refuge in the Tower of London, was effectively deposed for several days while the members of the coup quarreled over who was to succeed him. Unable to agree, they restored him to the throne but insisted on the dismissal of key ministers, some of whom were executed, and circumscribed his powers.

It took Richard ten years, but he played on the divisions among his opponents and slowly restored his power. In 1398, he struck back. Claiming that a group of nobles who included some of the Appellants were planning to assassinate him, he had several arrested and tried. One was executed; one banished; and the third, Richard's uncle, the duke of Gloucester, died under mysterious circumstances in Calais. It was generally assumed, then and now, that he had been murdered on Richard's orders. The play bears out this supposition early on, when Gaunt tells Gloucester's widow that justice for her husband's death must be left to God because no subject can revenge himself on the king.

Act I

Like most of Shakespeare's royal dramas, *Richard II* is at bottom a family story. The king is at its center at the beginning of the play, along with Richard's uncle, John of Gaunt, and John's son, Henry Bolingbroke. Bolingbroke is not just Richard's cousin. According to Nigel Saul, a biographer of Richard, there is evidence that Richard and Henry had been brought up together for part of their youth, and that Bolingbroke had been at Richard's side at important moments, including just before he confronted the mob during the Peasants' Rebellion. Also present at the drama's opening is Thomas Mowbray, another nobleman. Both Bolingbroke and Mowbray had been junior members of the Lords Appellant, who had conspired against Richard in the previous decade; but in the interim, they had been reconciled to him.

One of the king's roles was as judge and arbitrator of noble disputes, and it is in that role that Richard has called together Bolingbroke and Mowbray. Bolingbroke has accused Mowbray of killing the duke of Gloucester, as part of a pattern of treason. Unable to induce or even to order Bolingbroke and Mowbray to settle their quarrel, Richard assigns a day for them to meet in a trial by combat. Implicit in Richard's attempts to defuse the situation, for those who know the background of the story, is the assumption that since Richard was himself responsible for Gloucester's death, he had nothing to gain by an open discussion of the matter.

The actual trial by battle was a major political and sporting event. Both Bolingbroke and Mowbray sent abroad for new and expensive armor. Both brought a legion of friends and retainers to Coventry, where, Holinshed says, "The King caused a sumptuous scaffold or theatre" to be built from which he could witness the proceedings. When the combatants were mounted and about to clash, however, the king halted the contest. Neither Shakespeare nor the sources give a reason, but one speculation is that Richard not only wanted to close the case of Gloucester's death, he also wanted to avoid creating new divisions among the upper classes, who might divide into partisans of Bolingbroke or Mowbray if the conflict continued. After conferring with his senior advisers, Richard settled their dispute by banishing both, obviously favoring his cousin Bolingbroke by reducing his term, while Mowbray was banished for life. (Holinshed says of Mowbray that the king's failure to take his side "grieved him not a little," and that Mowbray ended up in Venice, "where he for thought and melancholy deceased.") The play dramatizes how, having pleased neither of the contenders, Richard prudently made them swear that they would have no contact with each other in their banishment.

Bolingbroke ended up in France, so well received by the king of France that he was offered the hand in marriage of the king's cousin, a match Richard used diplomatic pressure to prevent, referred to later in the play as one of the persecutions of Bolingbroke by Richard.

Act 2

A conversation between the dying Gaunt with his brother, the duke of York, gives Shakespeare the opportunity to review the failings of Richard's administration, and Gaunt's eloquent speech of how England ("this royal throne of kings, this scepter'd isle . . . this happy breed of men") has been ill-served by Richard's kingship. In particular, Gaunt cites Richard's decrees giving his cronies the power to "farm" or levy burdensome taxes. ("Now bound in with shame, with inky blots, and rotten parchment bonds.") With little left to lose, Gaunt chides Richard when he arrives with the statement that "A thousand flatterers sit within thy crown," and says that his grandfather Edward III, had he known the depths to which Richard's administration would sink, would have reached out "Deposing thee before thou wert possessed." Tellingly, Gaunt uses "thee" and "thou" to address Richard, which as a senior family member he is entitled to do, but the familiarity increases the sting of his criticisms, employing the voice one would use with an errant child.

Richard is not amused. "A lunatic, lean-witted fool," is how he describes his uncle, saying that if it were not for the fact that Gaunt is a son of Edward III, his statements "should run thy head from thy unreverent shoulders." Gaunt, noting that Gloucester's status as a son of Edward III did not prevent *his* death at Richard's hands, is carried off stage. ("Convey me to my bed, then to my grave.")

Richard's decision to seize Gaunt's estate and sell it off to raise money for his wars in Ireland, hinted at in the scene with his cronies before Gaunt's confrontation with him, is in many ways the turning point in the play. Another uncle, the long-suffering duke of York (brother of both Gaunt and Gloucester), cautions Richard against this action. "How art thou a king," York asks Richard, "but by fair sequence and succession?" He warns Richard that by wrongfully seizing the estate that now by rights belongs to Bolingbroke, "You pluck a thousand dangers on your head, you lose a thousand well-disposed hearts."

Historically, English kings had certain rights over the affairs of nobles. For instance, most proposed noble marriages were subject to his review, noble heirs were supposed to pay him a fee in order to collect their inheritance, and if a noble died without an obvious heir, his estate would be overseen by the king. Nor was it unheard of for a noble's estate to be taken over by the king in the wake of a great crime, such as treason. But for the king to seize Gaunt's huge estate and start selling it off to raise money posed a threat to the status of every noble family in the land. None could rest easy in his possessions, in constant fear that crossing the king could result in impoverishment – not only of themselves but of their descendents.

The conspiracy is hatched as soon as Richard has left the stage. The king, says Northumberland, "is basely led by flatterers," whose hatred of the nobles will lead Richard to "severely prosecute 'gainst us, our lives, our children and our heirs." But relief is almost in sight, as word has come that Bolingbroke (here referred to as Hereford) has left France, bound for England, "with eight tall ships, three thousand men of war." (In typical fashion, Shakespeare telescoped events. Gaunt died early in 1399 CE. It was months later before Bolingbroke left France.)

Shakespeare's principal source is Holinshed, who mentions the disagreement among his own sources about the size of Bolingbrook's expedition: estimates vary from fifteen lances to three thousand fighting men. But on his arrival at Ravenspurg in the northeast of England, "he was so joyfully received" by the local nobles that he soon had a significant force. Richard, meanwhile, was conducting his campaign in Ireland.

Bolingbroke's arrival, at least as far as the play is concerned, all but settles the issue. The duke of York, left in charge of England while Richard is in Ireland, looks to raise troops to repel Bolingbroke, only to be told that the most important lords of the north, the Percies, are already in the rebel camp. In the play, York complains that the forces he has raised to defeat Bolingbroke are weak, but Holinshed says the problem was that "there was not a man that would willingly thrust out one arrow at the duke of Lancaster," the title under which Bolingbroke began his invasion.

York urges Richard's intimates, Bushy, Bagot, and Green, who have profited so handsomely from the king's administration, to raise troops on their own, but they, believing the cause is already lost, flee for safety. In the next scene, York confronts Bolingbroke for ignoring his order of banishment and returning to England without the king's permission. Bolingbroke replies that he was banished as Hereford but returns as Lancaster, and "if that my cousin be King of England, it must be granted I am Duke of Lancaster." York's objections stated, he then invites Bolingbroke and his retinue into the castle he is holding.

Act 3

Act 3 begins with the dispatching of Bushy and Green, captured in the castle in which they had taken refuge. (Holinshed reports that "they had their heads smit off.") The next scene, that of Richard's arrival in England to defend his throne from Bolingbroke, takes Richard through a series of emotional states: elation to be back in England; despair to discover that his troops have dispersed; the recovery of his resolve to fight; and, finally, the realization that he has no hope of maintaining his throne, given the number of his important subjects who have flocked to Bolingbroke's standard. "Let us sit upon the ground," he says at one point, "and tell sad stories of the death of kings."

One of the underlying historical questions behind the scenes that follow is the degree to which Bolingbroke always intended to claim the crown, rather than simply his inheritance as the new duke of Lancaster. He had promised many of his followers that he sought no more than to remove the king's "evil" counselors and the recognition of his own right to inherit his father's estate, a position that would have found great sympathy among the other noble families. And, as we have seen, there was ample precedent even in Richard's reign for a strategy that would suspend or constrain most of the king's powers but leave him in place. Whether Bolingbroke began his invasion with

this end in mind or with the ultimate goal of gaining
the crown itself is an issue debated by historians.

Scene 3 dramatizes Richard's surrender, which is
much more drawn out in Holinshed's account. In
that version, the king was fortified in the castle at
Conway in Wales when Northumberland came to
him accompanied by only a few men and advanced a
proposal that a parliament be called that would judge
"against such as were enemies of the commonwealth
and had procured the destruction of the Duke of
Gloucester." Should this be done, Bolingbroke would
be "an humble subject" of Richard and ready to "obey
him in all dutiful services."

Richard agreed, and accompanied Northumberland.
Once on the road, however, Northumberland rode
ahead and rejoined the forces he had "hid closely in
two ambushes behind a craggy mountain" on the
highway. When the king rode into the ambush he
was captured and taken to the castle at Flint. There,
as Richard stood on the walls, Bolingbroke paraded
his whole army before the king's eyes. It was after this
display that the king came down from the walls of
the castle, met with Bolingbroke, and promised that
Bolingbroke might "enjoy all that is yours, without
exception."

The next scene – involving common gardeners and
the queen – brings the audience up to date on the
progress of the coup and introduces, through the voice
of the gardener, an overview of Richard's mistakes
and Bolingbroke's actions. However the royal
gardeners felt about their betters' politics, the scene
is an invention, particularly in terms of how it and
others portray Richard's first wife. Anne of Bohemia

had died in 1394 CE. Richard then became engaged to Isabella, the six-year-old daughter of the king of France, as part of a diplomatic initiative. She was only eleven or twelve years old when he was deposed.

Act 4

Echoing the start of the play, the act begins with a hearing, this time before parliament, filled with charges and countercharges around the death of the duke of Gloucester. Bolingbroke, now sitting in judgment, has no time to rule on the quarrel after the duke of York enters to announce that Richard has formally agreed to resign his office. It is the bishop of Carlisle who voices the most potent objections. "What subject can give sentence on his king?" he asks, and predicts that if Bolingbroke is crowned, "The blood of English shall manure the ground, and future ages groan for this foul act." For his pains, the bishop is immediately arrested for treason. (Shakespeare lifted much of Carlisle's speech directly from Holinshed, but he moved it to the deposition scene. In Holinshed, it is not made until after Bolingbroke was crowned in Richard's stead.)

Richard's elaborate public surrender of his office – however effective as drama – is not reflected in Holinshed's account. According to him, the king, a captive in the Tower of London, "being now in the hands of his enemies, and utterly despairing of all comfort, was easily persuaded to renounce his crown." The letter of resignation was read out in parliament, along with "33 solemn articles" that enumerated

Richard's "heinous points of misgovernment and injurious dealings."

The scene closes with Richard's departure and Bolingbroke's exit after having set the day for his coronation. Remaining on the stage are a group of conspirators: the abbot of Westminster, the bishop of Carlisle, and the duke of Aumerle, Richard's friend (and cousin of both Richard and Bolingbroke). Their conversation sets the stage for the end of the play and of Richard's life.

Act 5

Richard's leave-taking from his wife gives him yet another opportunity to bemoan his fate. He urges his wife Anne to return to France "from whence, she came adorned hither like sweet May," while he, instead of returning to the Tower, is banished to a castle in the north of England. Richard's wife at the time was Isabella, who, as noted earlier, was little more than a child. In fact she did return to France, where rather than join a nunnery as Richard urges in the play, she eventually married one of the most important figures in the land, the duke of Orleans.

The scenes involving Aumerle and his father the duke of York are drawn directly from Holinshed's account, as is the story of Aumerle's plea for mercy from King Henry for his involvement in the plot to assassinate him and return Richard to the throne. The duke of York's stern admonition that his son must pay the price of his treason – and the pleas of the duchess of York that he be pardoned – are not mentioned in Holinshed. He says only that Aumerle confessed to the king and that his father, arriving separately, "delivered the indenture that he had taken from his son."

According to Holinshed, when the conspirators gathered at Oxford and realized that Aumerle was missing they assumed that "their enterprise had been revealed to the King." They dressed a former clerk who resembled Richard in royal garb, to convince people that Richard had escaped, and took their forces to Windsor, only to find Henry not there. They eventually ended up in Cirencester, where they were defeated by Henry's troops. Shakespeare picks this up in Bolingbroke's conversation with York when he references the rebels at Cirencester (Ciceter in the text), followed by Northumberland's arrival to announce their defeat and the beheading of the principal conspirators.

It is, of course, Richard's continued presence that helped create the conspiracy. In the play, Sir Pierce Exton, a member of the court who has overheard the king asking for relief from the threat of Richard's existence, takes it upon himself to relieve King Henry of this burden. The details of Richard's battle with his assassins and his eventual death in the castle at Pontefract are drawn directly from Holinshed; King Henry's reaction and his rejection of Exton are not. As the play notes, Henry did resolve to go on crusade, but according to Holinshed it was years later, in 1413 CE, just before his death. Holinshed's (and Shakespeare's) story of Richard II's demise is not the only version of this event – other historical sources report that Richard was starved to death, not stabbed.

Afterthoughts

The deposition of a sitting king was a matter of great seriousness for chroniclers of the English monarchy, Shakespeare included. It is certainly true that the seeds of the Wars of the Roses, the civil war that raged during the tenure of Bolingbroke's grandson, Henry VI, were sown in Richard II's deposition. Shakespeare is thought to have written *Richard II* after composing the *Henry VI* plays, which portray that later conflict. It is sometimes assumed that the apocalyptic statements by the bishop of Carlisle, such as "The blood of English shall manure the ground," reflect Shakespeare's personal views, along with his dramatic approach.

Holinshed describes Richard II as "prodigal, ambitious and much given to the pleasure of the body," and claims that during his tenure "there reigned abundantly the filthy sin of lechery and fornication, with abominable adultery, specially in the King," a charge with which few modern chroniclers agree. Edward Hall, who wrote after the Wars of the Roses, takes pains to enumerate each of the 33 articles charged against the king in parliament, from "King Richard wastefully spent the treasure of the realm" to the duke of Gloucester's murder, right down to the allegation that Richard's diplomatic letters were "so subtle and so dark that no other prince durst once believe him, nor yet his own subjects."

Worth Noting

Act 5, scene 3 begins with a reference to Bolingbroke's son, Prince Hal, for whom the king asks that his aides inquire in the London taverns, which Hal "daily doth frequent with unrestrained loose companions." Hal's tavern habits and criminal associates are key plot issues in *Henry IV*, *Parts 1 and 2*, and the king's references to brothels was particularly appropriate for the Elizabethan stage, since it was not unusual for the theaters to be located in brothel districts.

Shakespeare's great predecessor in English letters, Geoffrey Chaucer, was a royal official during Richard II's reign and drew the characters in his works like *The Canterbury Tales* from this period. Chaucer's *The Book of the Duchess*, was about John of Gaunt's first wife, Blanche of Lancaster; Chaucer's own wife, Phillipa, was a sister of Gaunt's last wife, Kathryn Swynford; and Geoffrey and Phillipa's son, Thomas Chaucer, served a number of terms as Speaker of Parliament during later reigns.

For Further Viewing

There is a 1978 television version of *Richard II* starring Derek Jacobi as Richard II, with John Gielgud as John of Gaunt and Jon Finch as Henry Bolingbroke. A 1997 British television version features the actress Fiona Shaw as Richard II.

5

"Will Fortune never come with both hands full?"

Henry IV

In *Richard II*, Henry Bolingbroke, exiled by King Richard II and then denied his inheritance as duke of Lancaster, returned from France and deposed the unpopular Richard, making himself King Henry IV. But, as *Henry IV* shows, his reign was profoundly shaped by the method he had used to come to power. Emboldened by the fact that Henry had reached the throne illegitimately, Richard's adherents and other disaffected noble families fomented a series of rebellions. At the same time, Welsh rebels fought an ongoing guerilla war against the king's forces. Perhaps as a result of the stress of managing so much opposition, Henry spent much of his reign in ill health.

The Right of Succession

Primogeniture – the succession of the oldest son – was an established pattern of royal inheritance at this time. Edward III had come to the throne in 1327 by deposition, but he was already the heir of the monarch he replaced, his father. Bolingbroke's claim to the throne was far less solid. Like the man he deposed, Richard II, Henry Bolingbroke was a grandson of Edward III. But Richard was the oldest surviving son of Edward the Black Prince, himself the oldest son of Edward III, and thus Richard was much closer to the ideal of primogeniture.

Henry Bolingbroke was the offspring of Edward III's third surviving son, John of Gaunt. But even in Richard's absence he would not have been next in line under the rules of primogeniture as strictly applied. At the time of Richard's deposition, there were living descendants of Edward III's *second* son, Lionel. Technically, since Richard had no children, if the throne became vacant the person who should become king was one of Lionel's descendants, Edmund Mortimer. However, there were other issues. Mortimer was descended from Lionel's daughter rather than one of Lionel's sons. While the English were willing to recognize descent through the female line for Edward III's claim to the French throne (his mother was the sister of the deceased French king), they still preferred descent through the male line.

In addition, at the time of Henry's coup, Edmund Mortimer was only seven years old. The ruling class of England, having suffered under Richard after he had come to the throne at the age of ten, was not enthusiastic about another child monarch, however legitimate his claim. Another factor that recommended Bolingbroke to the nation's political elite in the effort to replace Richard (who was widely unpopular) was that Bolingbroke had four living sons, implying that succession issues were unlikely to arise again in the near future.

Wales

Wales makes up much of the south and west of the island that England occupies. The Anglo-Saxon invaders in the seventh and eighth centuries never managed to subdue the inhabitants, who retained their Celtic language, but in 1282 CE, the English King Edward I defeated a Welsh prince and established nominal English oversight of the territory. In 1301 CE, English sovereigns began naming their oldest son and heir the Prince of Wales, a tradition that continues to this day.

Owen Glendower was the son of a prominent Welsh family who had studied and practiced law in England ("I was trained up in the English court," he notes in act 3, scene 1), and who had served with English forces in Scotland. Capitalizing on Welsh resentment of English rule, he had himself crowned monarch of Wales early in Henry IV's reign. Glendower then used the mountainous terrain and stormy climate of Wales to tie up the English in a frustrating and expensive guerrilla war. He also made common cause with English nobles who opposed Henry IV.

Among those nobles were Henry Percy and his son, known as Hotspur, who were important landowners in the north of England. Early in Henry IV's tenure, the Percies defeated an invading Scottish force at Hamildon in Northumberland. However grateful Henry IV might have been for their defense of the realm, he managed to offend the Percies profoundly by insisting that their noble prisoners from the campaign be turned over to the crown. (It was the custom that such prisoners were the property of the actual winners of the battle, and their ransom was an important revenue source for their captors.)

The Percies eventually did turn over some of their prisoners, but not enough to satisfy Henry IV. Their disenchantment with Henry IV increased when he ignored their claims for funds to repay their military efforts on his behalf in Wales. They grew even unhappier when Henry refused to ransom a relative of theirs who had been captured in Wales defending Henry IV's interests. In 1403 CE, the younger Percy, Hotspur, led a rebellion against Henry IV that culminated in the battle of Shrewsbury near the Welsh border. Hotspur was killed during the battle, and the rebels were defeated.

Hotspur's father had taken no active part in the battle of Shrewsbury and so was pardoned by the king. But his opposition continued and, in 1408 CE, he led still another rebellion, this one defeated by Henry IV at Branham Moor. Glendower died, his rebellion eventually petered out, and the battle of Branham Moor marked the last major rebel military action. But Henry IV's health had been failing, and by this time was virtually broken. He died, aged forty-six, in 1413 CE.

Sir John Falstaff and Prince Hal's Wild Youth

The plays give only passing evidence of it, but the historical chroniclers are clear that Prince Hal, the future Henry V, played a prominent role in defending his father's crown, particularly in Wales. But there is another side to Prince Hal's youth, namely the stories of his "tavern keeping and low companions," to use his father's words in *Henry IV, Part 1*. It is difficult to know how realistic these stories were, but they were certainly in circulation in Shakespeare's time and entered into the folk history of the period.

The character of Sir John Falstaff requires a bit more elucidation. Falstaff's original name – according to early editions of the play as well as internal evidence – was Oldcastle. In one early scene, for instance, Hal makes a comment about "the old lad of the castle" in reference to him. In fact, there had been an Oldcastle in Henry IV's time, a soldier who had converted to Lollardy, a pre-Lutheran reform movement, and who had been executed for heresy. By Shakespeare's time, the Lollards had gone from being regarded as a historical footnote to being hailed as brave predecessors of English Protestantism. What's more, the Oldcastle family was still influential, and pressure was apparently brought to bear on Shakespeare to change the name. He chose a punning variant – Falstaff – on the name of a figure from the Hundred Years' War, Sir John Fastolf, and included a line in the epilogue to *Henry IV, Part 2*, that makes it clear that the character in question was not Oldcastle, "who died martyr."

Falstaff's charming roguery owes something to the medieval miracle and morality plays that were still being staged in Elizabethan times. These productions used Bible stories and other familiar tales to entertain and educate the populace, and one of the characters was traditionally the Vice, a figure that personified the dark side of human nature, often in a comic way. Shakespeare transformed the Vice, a stock theatrical construct, into an actual character, Falstaff, one of his most memorable creations.

Many of the history plays have brief comic scenes, but Falstaff and his companions represent the largest comic element in the histories. The other history plays focus heavily on the interaction between members of the upper classes, but Falstaff's presence gives the Henry IV plays the chance to portray life closer to the experience of Shakespeare's audience. As such they are a window – largely comic – into the life of the Elizabethan lower classes. Although the Henry IV plays are nominally set in the early 1400s, the scenes of tavern life reflect the period around 1600, and the issues and language would have been familiar to the groundlings who attended Shakespeare's theater.

Even though Sir John Falstaff is a knight and his language in the first play is full of classical allusions ("the chariot of Phoebus . . . Diana's foresters"), he is a rogue and his companions are scoundrels and thieves. His repeated references to thieves as subject to the "government" of the night and laboring in the "vocation" of theft are jibes at the obsession of Elizabethan authorities with assigning people to social and occupational roles and keeping them there.

Part 1

The first scene sets the political situation. Wales is in rebellion under Glendower, and the Welsh have defeated and captured the earl of March, Lord Mortimer. There is also good news. The king's then-allies in the north, the Percies (the senior Percy was the earl of Northumberland, his brother the earl of Worcester), joined by Percy's son Henry, have defeated an invasion by the Scots at Hamildon. The king envies the senior Henry Percy his son, Hotspur, "the theme of honor's tongue" and compares Hotspur to his own son Hal, whose brow is stained by "riot and dishonor." Because the Henry IV plays are about Hal's transformation from a feckless youth into a great king, Shakespeare ignores the record of Hal's military exploits, along with the fact that Hotspur was older not only than the king's "young Harry," he was actually older than King Henry himself.

Our introduction to Falstaff involves the plan for robbing a group of pilgrims and traders at Gad's Hill (east of London on the road to Canterbury). There is a great deal of jesting about the subject, but for Falstaff and most of his companions it could be a deadly serious business. Elizabethans had jails for those awaiting trial on serious charges, but no prisons in our current sense. While Falstaff and Hal may joke about it, Shakespeare's audience knew that the penalty for serious felonies like armed robbery was hanging – public executions were an amusement that competed with Elizabethan playhouses for audiences. Renowned historical Shakespearean A. L. Rowse noted in his book, *The England of Elizabeth*, that in the county of Devon alone in 1598, seventy-four people were executed for various felonies. Yet the administration of justice was irregular at best. Rowse notes, "[Y]ou were liable to be hanged or get off scot-free" because juries of common people were reluctant to impose unduly harsh punishments, particularly for a crime against property.

The next scene lays out the quarrel between the Percies and the king and includes the king's refusal to ransom from Glendower Lord Mortimer. Like his sources, Shakespeare confuses the hostage Mortimer with his nephew, the boy who under the strict interpretation of royal lineage had a stronger claim to the throne than did King Henry IV. The potential pretender Mortimer and his brother were – while very well treated – effectively King Henry IV's prisoners during this period.

Hotspur's description of "Richard that sweet lovely rose" and his successor, "this thorn, this canker, Bolingbroke," ignores the almost universal disdain for Richard at the time of his deposition. The earl of Worcester urges caution and dissimulation to achieve the same end that Hotspur was about to recommend: "to bear our fortunes in our own strong arms" in rebellion against Henry IV, in league with Glendower. They are to be joined by Mortimer, who as a prisoner had switched sides and married Glendower's daughter, and by the Scots, ever interested in anything that would destabilize the English crown.

Elizabethan Details

The play goes back and forth between scenes of the high life – the doings of the nobles – and the low, namely the Elizabethan taverns. While certainly downmarket when compared to the king's table, taverns were actually a bit more upscale than Elizabethan alehouses, because taverns offered food cooked on the premises (inns were even more upscale and offered rooms for overnight stays). Ale – essentially beer without hops – was the regular drink of English men and women, since water was often of doubtful quality, particularly in densely occupied places like London. The "sack" that Falstaff repeatedly calls for was the Elizabethan name for sherry, the sweet Spanish wine that the English made even sweeter with sugar, which Hal mentions in his discussion with Poins. The "tapsters" and "drawers" are employees of the tavern.

Elizabethan money is a complicated issue, and even when adjusted for four hundred years' worth of inflation very difficult to compare with our currency. For one thing, Elizabethans probably paid a much larger share of their income for food than we do today, while all but the rich had far fewer clothes, and those often homemade. Falstaff mentions the "thousand pounds" gained and then lost from the robbery at Gad's Hill. This was a very considerable amount, particularly when one considers that 10 to 15 pounds a year might keep an entire rural family well above the poverty line.

The fact that Falstaff is overweight ("a gross fat man," says the sheriff; "a goodly, portly man," says

Falstaff of himself) is a reflection of his income as well as his habits. Most people in England could not afford to eat enough to be seriously overweight. A workingman might earn fourpence a day in wages (sometimes including food), while the bill for dinner that Hal finds in Falstaff's pocket included fourpence for sauce alone, an entire chicken (at 26 pence) and more than eight shillings (at 12 pence per shilling) principally for fancy imported wine. Falstaff's bill for a single meal thus roughly equals a workingman's monthly wage – a fact that would not have been lost on the working-class audience standing closest to the Elizabethan stage.

Act 3

This section begins with some verbal jostling among the members of the rebel alliance – Mortimer, Hotspur and Glendower – as they sit down to divide the country among themselves. Holinshed says the meeting happened in the house of the Archdeacon in Bangor in Wales, where the conspirators' deputies "divided the realm amongst them, causing a tripartite indenture to be made and sealed with their seals."

"I can call spirits from the vasty deep," says Glendower, while Hotspur responds, "Why, so can I, or so can any man. But will they come when you do call for them?" Their disagreement over the division (when Hotspur calls for the rerouting of a river to equalize their territory, "I'll not have it so," Glendower responds) indicates that their alliance is not on the most stable ground.

Meanwhile, back in the king's court, Henry IV berates Hal for his riotous ways and compares him unfavorably to Hotspur, who "leads ancient lords and reverend bishops on to bloody battles and to bruising arms" while Hal has become "my nearest and dearest enemy." Here Hal promises to transform himself. "I shall make this northern youth exchange his glorious deeds for my indignities," he says, promising to die "a hundred thousand deaths ere break the smallest parcel of this vow." Replies his relieved father, "a hundred thousand rebels die in this," and the king gives him a command of troops for the upcoming Battle of Shrewsbury.

Hal immediately offers Falstaff a similar chance at redemption. He tells Falstaff that he is putting him in command of "a charge of foot" or infantry for the coming battle and orders Falstaff to meet him the next day, where he will be given "money and order" for their recruitment. Under the English system of the time, commanders were paid a lump sum to recruit, equip, and maintain a company of soldiers (and Falstaff will demonstrate how an unethical commander could make money out of the process).

Falstaff's military history is never made clear in the play, but knighthood was not an inherited condition. It was an honor generally awarded to middle- and upper-class individuals, usually those who had distinguished themselves on the battlefield. In the second part of *Henry IV*, one of the characters mentions that Falstaff had been a page to Thomas Mowbray, the duke of Norfolk, who undertook military campaigns on behalf of Richard II before being banished. Young aides to such leaders were sometimes knighted, either in response to their bravery in action or before a battle, to strengthen their resolve. Whereas Falstaff is an invented figure, Mowbray, the first duke of Norfolk, is a real historical character; however, it is unlikely that Falstaff – if he existed – could have been his page. Mowbray was a generation younger than Falstaff (who admits to being fifty, a considerable age at the time, but he is probably older), and any of Mowbray's pages would probably have been younger than Mowbray himself.

When Hal meets Falstaff before the battle, he remarks on the "pitiful rascals" Falstaff has put together for his company. By Falstaff's own admission, he has conscripted "none but good householders, yeomen's sons" and other young men who were eager to avoid service and who had enough money to bribe their way out (and Falstaff has some 300 pounds to show for his strategy). Having let the best candidates evade the draft, Falstaff has assembled "a hundred and fifty tattered prodigals . . . most of them out of prison." He tells Hal his men are "food for powder . . . they'll fill a pit (a grave) as well as better." Falstaff's repeated references to gunpowder, muskets, and pistols are ahistorical and refer to warfare in Shakespeare's time. In 1403 CE – the date of the Battle of Shrewsbury – handheld gunpowder weapons were not in common use.

Outside Shrewsbury, meanwhile, Hotspur learns that his father, the earl of Northumberland, is sick and will not be joining the rebels. Undeterred, he decides to proceed, on the logic that the absence of his father's forces "lends a luster and more great opinion, a larger dare to our great enterprise."

The accounts of the proceedings before the battle and of the battle itself are drawn largely from Holinshed (embroidered by the doings of Falstaff). They include the king's offer of pardon that Worcester never conveyed to the rest of the rebels, along with the fact that a number of knights were dressed to appear to be the king in order to confuse their opponents. Holinshed reports that "the Prince that day holp his father like a lusty young gentleman" and refused to leave the field though wounded by an arrow to the face. Hotspur was killed in the battle, but the scene where Hal kills him is Shakespeare's invention. "Thus ever did rebellion find rebuke," remarks King Henry IV after the victory, ignoring the fact that his own rebellion against King Richard ended a good deal more happily for himself and *his* rebels.

Part 2, Acts 1 and 2

The sequel opens with a reminder to the audience of what occurred in the last play. The news is brought to Hotspur's father, the earl of Northumberland, of the deaths of Hotspur and the earl's brother, Worcester. The spirit of rebellion lives on, however, in the Archbishop of York, Richard Scroop. The archbishop was one of the churchmen who swore in Henry as king but now he "has turned insurrection to religion," Northumberland remarks. According to Holinshed, the archbishop, appearing in armor among his flock, promised "forgiveness of sins to all of them whose hap it was to die in the quarrel" with the king, and "the gravity of his age, his integrity of

life and incomparable learning" drew followers to
him and the rebel cause.

At the forest of Gaultree the rebels – once again
without the forces of Northumberland – debate
whether to proceed against the king's troops, led this
time by Prince John (Hal's brother) and Westmoreland.
In Shakespeare's version, Archbishop Scroop tells the
group that "the commonwealth is sick of their choice"
of Henry as king: "They that when Richard was alive
would have him die are now enamoured of his grave."
According to the story Northumberland hears, the
archbishop should be numbered among them, for the
churchman "doth enlarge his rising with the blood
of Richard scraped from Pomfret stones." (Pomfret
Castle was where Richard died.) Northumberland's
location becomes clear in scene 3. After discussions
with his wife and his son's widow he decides not
to join Scroop's rebellion, but to head for safety in
Scotland.

Act 3 begins with the sleepless king ("uneasy lies
the head that wears a crown," he says of himself). The
rumor of Northumberland's defection reminds him of
Richard's comment about Northumberland, to whom
Richard had entrusted the kingdom while he was on
campaign in Ireland. Richard predicted that because
Northumberland had switched sides once, he was
likely to do so again. But the news is not all bad. On
the Welsh front, it appears that Glendower is dead.

Shakespeare intersperses these historical scenes
with comic relief in the form of Falstaff and his
companions, generally engaged in a combination of
drinking, arguing, and fighting, interrupted at one
point by the appearance of the law in the form of

two sergeants and the Lord Chief Justice. The perspicacity of the Chief Justice contrasts with the later scenes and with the less insightful justices of the peace in the countryside, Shallow and Silence. Although they are comic figures, their roles illustrate the form of government administration outside London. Justices of the Peace were empowered to settle local disputes and carried out various other administrative duties, in this case producing from the locality a group of potential draftees for the king's forces (the most likely of whom, as in *Part 1*, immediately bribe Falstaff and his lieutenant, Bardolph, to escape service).

The scenes with Justice Shallow also fill out our picture of Falstaff's past. According to Shallow, the two were students at Clement's Inn, a minor law school, where at least by Shallow's account their time was spent in drinking, brawling, and whoring. Shakespeare's audience would have no trouble recognizing such an account of law-student life. Shallow's lack of attention to his studies would not have been a handicap in his current role because local justices were not expected to have a legal education.

The name Thomas Mowbray, which first appeared in this cycle of the history plays in the opening scenes of *Richard II*, resurfaces at this point in the person of one of the rebel leaders. The first Thomas Mowbray's dispute with Henry Bolingbroke led to the banishment of both himself and Bolingbroke by Richard II. But while Bolingbroke had returned to claim his dukedom and the crown, Mowbray senior had died in Venice. The earl of Westmoreland, confronting the rebels at the forest of Gaultree, doubts that this second Mowbray has "an inch of ground to build a grief on," against

Henry IV because the king had overlooked his quarrel with Mowbray's father and restored the younger Mowbray "to all the Duke of Norfolk's signories." Westmoreland accuses all the leaders, including the "reverend father" archbishop, of dressing "the ugly form of base and bloody insurrection with your fair honors."

Having learned that Northumberland will not be joining them, the rebels, led by Archbishop Scroop, decide to believe the representations of Westmoreland and Prince John that their grievances will be addressed. Mowbray fears that the king will eventually turn on them, but they are all astonished to find that once they have demobilized their troops they are taken into custody. Says Holinshed, "the Archbishop perceived not that he was deceived until the earl of Westmoreland arrested both him and the earl Marshal with diverse others."

Prince John says in response to their accusations of treachery, "I promised you redress of these same grievances . . . which, by mine honor I will perform with most Christian care. But for you, rebels, look to taste the due meet for rebellion and such acts as yours." In fact, the rebel leaders, including Archbishop Scroop, were later beheaded at York. Holinshed adds, "The Archbishop suffered death very constantly, insomuch as the common people took it he died a martyr."

The play has Falstaff more or less capturing the rebel Sir John Coleville of the Dale. The incident was probably inspired by Holinshed's account of the rebellion, though Holinshed says only that Coleville was executed at Durham after "being convicted of the conspiracy." Coleville's death actually came after the king himself mounted an expedition against Northumberland in 1405 CE.

In the next scene, Shakespeare telescopes the action, as Henry IV is informed not only of the victory at Gaultree (in 1405 CE) but also of Northumberland's eventual defeat (in 1408 CE at the Battle of Branham Moor). In the play, the increasingly ill Henry asks, "Will Fortune never come with both hands full?" given the declining state of his health. Gloucester notes that "the river hath thrice flowed, no ebb between," which supposedly had previously occurred just before the death of Edward III (the river is the Thames, and the portent taken from Holinshed).

The chroniclers mention serious discord between the king and Prince Hal in Henry's final years, particularly as Henry's ill health reduced his capacity to govern. The writer John Stow (working from earlier sources) says that at one point Prince Hal came to the king and offered him a dagger to use on him if the king believed the stories that were being told about Hal's ambitions. A similar reconciliation occurs in the play, but later, when Hal finds his father apparently dead and takes away his crown. According to Holinshed, Hal was not the only one who believed that Henry was dead, since the king's attendants had covered his face with a linen cloth. In Holinshed's account, as opposed to Shakespeare's, their interaction at that point was very brief, with the king commending Hal to God.

The play makes much of Henry's preparations for a Crusade to the Holy Land (he had visited there as a young man), presumably because Shakespeare wanted to highlight Henry's belief in a prophecy that he would die in Jerusalem. According to Holinshed, Henry's health had improved sufficiently for him to plan such an expedition, but he took a turn for the worse after Christmas of 1412 CE. Apparently, his final illness came upon him suddenly, and his attendants "bare him into a chamber that was next at hand belonging to the Abbot of Westminster," says Holinshed. He died March 21, 1413 CE, in that room, known from biblical hangings on its walls as "the Jerusalem chamber."

Hal's Accession

A little more than two weeks later, Hal was crowned Henry V. According to Holinshed, he chose for his advisers men of "gravity, wit and high policy," although previously he had "made himself a companion of misruly mates of dissolute order and life." The details of Hal's previous lifestyle are as much legend as history, and Shakespeare's version of these events seems to owe a great deal to a roughly contemporaneous play called *The Famous Victories of Henry V.* However, Holinshed does cite one incident of Hal's youth, noting how, after one of his men had been sent to prison, Hal had "with his fist stricken the Chief Justice." But Holinshed also notes that when the justice then sent Hal to prison, "he (the Prince) obeyed."

This story was the source of act 5, scene 2, where the Chief Justice and the new king meet. The justice, anticipating the worst, says, "If truth and upright innocence fail me, I'll to the King my master that is dead, and tell him who has sent me after him." But

Henry V, reinforcing the legend of his reformation, greets the Chief Justice as "the father to my youth" and confirms him in his post. Should Henry's own offspring need such correction as the Chief Justice meted out to him, says Henry V, "Happy am I, that have a man so bold that dares to do justice on my proper son."

The scene where Henry V turns his back on Falstaff ("I know thee not, old man,") dramatizes Holinshed's comment on Hal's attitude toward his former companions: "He banished them all from his presence (but not unrewarded or else unpreferred), inhibiting them upon a great pain not once to approach, lodge or sojourn within ten miles of his court or presence."

In the play, Sir John and companions are taken off to prison by order of the Chief Justice. The epilogue closes with the declaration that "our humble author will continue the story, with Sir John in it," but Falstaff does not appear in *Henry V*, although there is a scene that recounts his death.

Reconciliation

Among Henry V's first acts was to offer a truce to the remaining Welsh rebels, who accepted. He also began the rehabilitation process for Richard II. As Bolingbroke's son, Hal had been in effect held hostage by Richard II for his banished father's behavior. But Richard had treated Hal well, even after his father had begun the rebellion that led to Richard's deposition. As Henry V, he had Richard's remains disinterred from a church in Hertfordshire and reburied in Westminster Cathedral, the traditional burial site for English kings. (The reburial also served to remind potential rebels that – any rumors to the contrary – Richard II was dead and unavailable for restoration to his throne.)

For Further Viewing

The 1979 BBC version of these plays features Anthony Quayle as Falstaff, with Jon Finch as Henry IV and David Gwillim as Prince Hal. The actor–director Orson Welles also made Falstaff his own with *Chimes at Midnight*, a 1965 film that combines scenes from all the plays in which Falstaff appears.

6

"God fought for us"

Henry V

The so-called Hundred Years' War is generally regarded as having begun in 1337 CE, when England's King Edward III went to war in France. The previous French king had died without a son to succeed him, and Edward III, whose mother was the dead king's sister, felt that as a nephew he had as much right as any other claimant. Part of the original focus of the war was a dispute over Gascony in southern France, an area that had been in the English sphere of influence for more than one hundred and fifty years, thanks to the marriage of Eleanor of Aquitaine, whose family ruled the territory, to the king of England, Henry II (see *King John*).

The Battle of Crecy, in which English archers defeated a much larger force of French knights, was the most dramatic event of those early years of the war. A decade later, at the Battle of Poitiers, the English captured the then king of France and his son, along with "seventeen earls, besides barons, knights and squires, and slain five or six thousand," according to the chronicler Jean Froissart. King Edward III's son, Edward the Black Prince, was among the principal English campaigners of these years. The war eventually wound down, in part because later English kings had other priorities. The Black Prince's son, Richard II, who inherited the throne when his father and grandfather died, tried to reach an accommodation with France, preferring to focus his energies on stabilizing the political situation in Ireland. Richard's usurper and successor Henry IV, like Richard, had little interest in fights between Christian kings. He had to battle rebellions in Wales and England and eventually hoped to lead a crusade to the Holy Land, although he died before the expedition could be mounted.

But on his accession to the throne, Henry V, the son of Henry IV, felt the time was right to reassert Edward III's claims and to rekindle the French campaign.

France in 1415

Henry V's strategy of reasserting his predecessor's territorial claims in France was predicated in part on the divisions that then existed among the French nobility. Charles VI was nominally king of France, but his actual power was diluted by that of his nobles. They theoretically owed him allegiance but often acted as independent rulers of their territories and quarreled incessantly among themselves. The principal antagonism was between the Burgundians and the Armagnacs, both of whom sought to control the crown. Making things even more complicated was the fact that Charles VI had a mental disorder that made him ineffective for long periods. Henry V's military successes at the Battle of Agincourt and in his later campaigns owed a great deal to Charles VI's inability to govern, and to the fact that the Burgundians – who controlled much of northwest France and the Low Countries – stayed largely on the sidelines during Henry V's campaigns in France.

Henry V and Parliament

Henry IV, who had seized power in a coup d'état, had been dogged, as noted, by internal rebellions and had a difficult relationship with parliament, which had to approve taxes for military expeditions. One of the remarkable traits of Henry V was his ability to unite the country, after decades of weak and controversial leadership under Richard II and Henry IV. Within two years of his accession, he managed to get parliament to agree to a series of special levies, then oversaw the recruiting, equipping, and transporting of a major army for a foreign campaign.

The Longbow

The decisive weapon of the Battle of Crecy and (we shall see) at Agincourt, was the English longbow. The Normans seemed to have learned the use of the longbow from the Welsh, who took a heavy toll on the invaders in the battles that accompanied their pacification of Wales after the Norman conquest of 1066 CE. Welsh bowmen were afterwards incorporated into English forces, and English kings encouraged archery among their male subjects.

Longbows ranged from about five feet to more than six feet in length (taller than most English men of that time), and they could fire heavy arrows some two hundred yards or farther. The arrows could penetrate all but the heaviest armor then in use and were particularly effective against horses, which were generally much more lightly armored than their riders. Although effective at close range, the longbows' strategic importance came from the fact that they could be fired in volleys, like modern artillery, and could break a massed charge of armored knights.

Many continental armies at the time relied on crossbowmen. But the longbow had longer range, greater accuracy, and a higher rate of fire. Its principal disadvantage was that it took great strength and years of practice to master. A second disadvantage was that longbowmen also wore little or no armor, so that if the enemy managed to get through the storm of arrows, the archers were very vulnerable. They often fought behind barricades made of sharpened stakes stuck in the ground at an angle to resist a cavalry charge.

The Play

The drama begins not with Henry V but with two churchmen debating the threatened passage of a bill that would heavily tax church property. At this time, the Roman Catholic Church owned or controlled perhaps as much as one-third of the land in England and would do so until Henry VIII broke up the monasteries more than one hundred years later. A similar bill had been introduced in parliament near the end of Henry IV's reign, and the churchmen decide that offering to support an invasion of France will effectively kill the measure. (Few historians believe that it was the church's sudden provision of funds that got Henry interested in invading France, though the church did make a special financial effort on the campaign's behalf.)

Picking up a theme introduced in the two preceding *Henry IV* plays, the bishops discuss the change in Henry's character upon assuming the crown. "The breath no sooner left his father's body but that his wildness, mortified in him, seemed to die too," remarks one and contrasts it with Henry's current condition, "full of grace and fair regard." Says the Archbishop of Canterbury, "Hear him but reason in divinity . . . you would desire the King were made a prelate. . . . Hear him debate of commonwealth affairs, you would say it hath been all in all his study . . . turn him to any cause of policy, the Gordian knot of it he will unloose."

The policy of reclaiming supposedly English lands in France was high on Henry's agenda, and the play quotes extensively from Holinshed on the French legal objections to Henry's – actually Edward III's – claim. Shakespeare plays the scene for laughs, with a detailed refutation of the French legal position, including references to the legendary King Pharamond of the Franks and the ninth-century European leader Charlemagne.

The audience is further reminded of Henry's playboy reputation by the account of the Dauphin's mocking present of tennis balls, a story taken from Holinshed. The predecessor of modern lawn tennis, court tennis was at the time a rich man's game played in enclosed courts by the upper classes, including royalty.

Act 2 begins with the Chorus saying, "Now all the youth of England are on fire . . . and honor's thought reigns solely in the breast of every man," as the nation prepares for war. But Shakespeare sets the first scene in the London street, and the characters are those whose concept of honor is irregular at best.

Nym, Pistol, and Bardolph, along with Mistress Quickly and the pageboy, are characters carried over from the *Henry IV* plays, members of the circle around the charming rogue Sir John Falstaff. The men's empty bragging and ceaseless quarreling over insults to their honor create a comic mirror to the disputes among their betters. Shakespeare had promised in the close of *Henry IV, Part 2*, to bring back the character of Falstaff, but in *Henry V* he is never seen, only referred to, and his death scene occurs completely offstage.

Scene 2 is set in Southhampton, where Henry V has created a fleet to carry his army to France. The story of the three conspirators who planned to murder Henry, as set up by Chorus in the prologue, is taken largely from Holinshed, who indicates that their plot was sponsored and paid for by the king of France. However, Shakespeare ignores other information from Holinshed that makes the plot somewhat more complicated. According to Holinshed, the Earl of Cambridge participated because he believed Henry's death would lead to the crowning of the rightful heir,

Edmund Mortimer (see the chapter on *Henry IV* for a more extensive discussion of Mortimer's claim to the throne). Edmund Mortimer was Cambridge's brother-in-law, and Mortimer (says Holinshed) "for diverse secret impediments" was not able to have children. Cambridge apparently believed that if Mortimer became king, after his death the crown would revert to Cambridge's family because Cambridge's sons, as Mortimer's nephews, would become Mortimer's heirs. Holinshed does not discuss how the plot was revealed. According to other historians, Mortimer himself brought it to Henry V, and Henry absolved him of all blame in connection with it.

The Average Soldier

Although Henry V was interested in recovering what he believed to be his patrimony, and many of his nobles were members of a military caste who wanted to prove their martial abilities, the average soldier on such an expedition had largely economic motives. There was no standing army, so the archers who made up the bulk of the forces were men with other occupations. Skilled workmen in England who made three to five pence a day, out of which they often had to buy their own food, could make sixpence a day on an expedition, with food provided by the king. In addition, there was always the opportunity for booty from captured cities or slain enemies, which explains Pistol's act 2, scene 3 comparison of his companions to "horse-leeches" as they depart for France "to suck, to suck the very blood."

Shakespeare sets the final diplomatic discussion before the invasion in the French court. The king, the dauphin, and their counselors argue about what steps to take to repel the English when Exeter, a messenger from Henry V, arrives to tell them to surrender or face the grief of "the widows' tears, the orphans' cries, the dead men's blood, the pining maidens' groans" that will result from their war. In Holinshed's account, this meeting took place in England, where French ambassadors promised Henry the hand of Catherine and a "great sum of money," along with certain territories, if he would disband his army. It was the Archbishop of Canterbury who replied that if the French king did not agree to all of Henry's demands he would "with all diligence enter France and destroy the people, waste the country and subvert the towns with blood, sword and fire."

Harfleur

Henry's chosen invasion point was Harfleur, a port city at the mouth of the Seine, the river that led to Rouen and eventually Paris. Harfleur had been the home port of the French and mercenary raiders who had been preying on English shipping, and its capture would eliminate much of that threat. In addition, Harfleur's capture, along with the longtime English occupation of Calais further up the coast, would permit the English to operate two bases that could reinforce each other, and give Henry a stronger hand to negotiate with the various power centers in France.

The characters Fluellen, Jamy, and MacMorris – military engineers who stand for the Welsh, Scot, and Irish members of Henry V's army, respectively – offer Shakespeare the chance to explain siege tactics and to emphasize the unity of the kingdom. Set-piece battles between large armies, while they did occur, were not a major part of medieval warfare, including the Hundred Years' War. Until the use of cannon was perfected, the average medieval battle was the siege of a walled town or castle. One of the principal siege tactics was to dig mines underneath a key point in the walls, then to set fire to the timbers that held up the roof of these man-made caves. The resulting collapse of the mine would destabilize the castle walls or even bring them down.

The countermines Fluellen mentions in the dialogue with his fellow engineer officers were a defensive tactic. Defenders would dig mines under those being dug by their attackers, and collapse them and the mines above before the attackers reached the walls. Sometimes those digging the mines and countermines met, leading to battles underground.

The defense of Harfleur proved stubborn. Henry's troops arrived in the middle of August, but by late September the town was still holding out. In the play, the citizens surrender after Henry promises them they will see "the blind and bloody soldier with foul hand defile the locks of your shrill-shrieking daughters, your fathers taken by their silver beards and their most reverend heads dashed to the walls, your naked infants spitted upon pikes." Sieges were a regular part of warfare in the Middle Ages, and an entire protocol had evolved around them. In this case, the citizens of

Harfleur had sent emissaries – permitted by Henry V to go through his lines – to determine whether and when the city could expect reinforcements. When the dauphin informed them that they could expect no immediate help, the city surrendered to Henry's forces. In the play, the king tells Exeter to "use mercy to them all," and while Henry did enforce discipline among his occupying troops, the residents were eventually evicted from the city and escorted into territory controlled by the French. Henry left a garrison to hold the town and soon moved on, telling Exeter that "The winter coming on, and sickness growing upon our soldiers, we will retire to Calais."

Act 3, scene 4 is a conversation between Princess Catherine of France and her maid almost completely in French. It is an elaborate smutty joke on the aural resemblance between French vulgarisms and the English words "foot" and "gown."

The Road to Calais

Henry had lost perhaps half his forces to dysentery during the siege. Men either died or had to be sent home because they were too ill to fight. He could have simply returned to England as the victor over Harfleur, but his ambition was to win significant French territory – or to at least to establish a better claim to ownership of it. That led him to embark on a dangerous journey across northern France. By now, Henry must have known that the French had had enough time to overcome both their internal divisions and the logistical problems that made assembling a medieval military army so difficult. He must have fully expected to face a significant force that would try to block his path to Calais, and that is precisely what happened.

Henry's troops followed a roughly northeastern route, parallel to the coastline, but were stymied at the River Somme. They ended up having to the follow the river into the interior before they found a lightly guarded crossing point. But shortly after accomplishing the crossing, Henry was approached by French heralds who offered him – in the noble tradition – the chance to set a date and place for a battle. He told them that while he did not seek a battle he was willing to fight one, and that the French knew where to find him.

Shakespeare's version of this incident has Henry receive the herald of the French king. In his master's name, Montjoy demands what ransom Henry will offer for his own life, "which must proportion for the losses we have borne, the subjects we have lost, the disgrace we have digested," adding that Henry had "betrayed his followers, whose condemnation is pronounced." The question of ransom emerges several times in the play. It was the custom for noble prisoners captured in battle to be offered the chance to ransom their lives. This system applied as far down as knights and esquires, if their families had money. But it was an understandable source of discord in the armies of the period that losers of a battle had a chance to survive if they were noble, whereas all other prisoners were generally executed by the winners. Henry's assurance to Montjoy, the French herald, that "my ransom is this frail and worthless trunk," is meant to demonstrate his courage and resolve, and his willingness to suffer the potential fate of his ordinary soldiers.

Heralds played a particular role in the protocol of jousts and war itself. They served not only as messengers between the parties, but also as umpires and even judges. It would be up to a herald, for instance, in some circumstances to decide which party had won a joust. So while Mountjoy was French, his office was that of an intermediary, and he did not take sides in the conflict. In the play, Henry not only compliments Montjoy about how he does his job, he gives the herald a purse for his services.

The Night before the Battle

In the scene with Montjoy, Henry admits that "my people are with sickness much enfeebled, my numbers lessened." A force several times the size of Henry's army established itself across his route to Calais. The play lays out the strategic situation the night before the battle. The French troops – rested and fully equipped – heavily outnumber the English, many of them ill and worn down by the previous siege and by days of struggle on the primitive roads. The greatest worry the French have is that there will not be enough English to put up a decent fight. The spokesman in the play for this fear is the dauphin, but Shakespeare notes in a previous scene that the king had ordered the dauphin not to take part in the battle. In fact, he was not there.

The armies were so close that they not only could see each other's fires, at some points they also could overhear one another's conversations, leading to Captain Fluellen's upbraiding of Gower, his fellow officer, for talking too loudly. Henry's tour of his positions, concealed in a cloak, gives Shakespeare the opportunity to defend the roles of both king and commoner in such conflicts ("Every subject's duty is the King, but every subject's soul is his own.") Once the soldiers have left, Henry's soliloquy echoes his father's troubled mind in the *Henry IV* plays ("What infinite hearts-ease must kings neglect that private men enjoy . . ."), and he asks God to "think not upon the fault my father made" when he usurped the crown of Richard II. As noted earlier, Henry V had reinterred the murdered Richard's body from a church outside of London to Westminster Abbey. He notes in the soliloquy that he has bestowed on it "more contrite tears than from it issued forced drops of blood."

The Day of the Battle

Westmoreland's wish, "that we now had here but one ten thousand of those men in England who do no work today," is taken from Holinshed (though Holinshed does not record who said it), as is Henry's response, "I would not wish a man more here than I have." Henry's famous speech, "We few, we happy few, we band of brothers," is a good deal shorter and less oratorical in Holinshed: "But be you of good comfort, and show yourselves valiant, God and our just quarrel shall defend us."

The absolute size of Henry's army – and of the French host – has been the subject of much speculation. Estimates of Henry's force vary from about six thousand to perhaps twelve thousand, depending on whether noncombatants are counted. The French certainly outnumbered Henry by a factor of three and perhaps by as much as a factor of six. Unmentioned by Shakespeare, except in passing in Henry's description of his troops' "muddy marching," was the fact that it had been raining heavily, and that the rain continued all night before the battle, creating a huge tactical advantage for the English. The French had arrayed themselves across a front of about a thousand yards. The English had a small village at their backs, and heavy woods at their right and left. Before them was a field that had been soaking in the rain.

The size of forces, while important, is not the most critical factor in military strategy, as both Henry and the French understood. Henry's force was small enough, and its position compact enough, to make communication relatively easy. In addition, Henry's troops had been together for months, and Henry was the clear leader, supported by his brother and other nobles. The French force, like many medieval armies, was completely ad hoc, having come together solely for this battle, and without clear lines of leadership. In the absence of the king and the dauphin, the leadership was shared among a number of royal dukes and the Constable of France, and decisions about strategy were negotiated compromises designed to give all the important players a prominent role. Every noble wanted a leading part in what the French believed would be a battle where victory was all but assured.

When the battle was joined, the effects of the weather became immediately clear. A cloud of English arrows broke up the charge of the French armored knights. Horses and men fell, wounded or killed by arrows, and floundered in the mud, slowing or stopping the knights behind them, who became new targets for English longbowmen. The dismounted French knights and men-at-arms, struggling in the mud and slowed down by their heavy armor, were vulnerable to the much more mobile English archers. When they ran out of arrows, the archers attacked them with knives and axes designed to penetrate helmet visors or the joints between sheets of plate armor.

The lack of central leadership made it difficult for the French to keep additional knights from pushing into the fray and adding to the fatal confusion. Meanwhile, the woods and hedges on either side of the English prevented the French from making a massed attack of infantry or cavalry that could have rolled up one of the English flanks.

At one point, a party of French cavalry penetrated English lines and attacked the baggage train, killing the boys who were left to guard it. At another point, Henry, fearing a resurgence of the French, ordered all French prisoners taken so far to be executed – "pity it was to see how some Frenchmen were sticked with daggers, some were brained with poleaxes," says Holinshed.

Holinshed also reports that about 4:00 in the afternoon, with the French dead in heaps about the field, "the King when he saw no appearance of enemies, caused the retreat to be blown; and gathering his army together, gave thanks to almighty God for so happy a victory." In the play, Montjoy arrives at this point to perform his office and to inform the English they have won the day. Other historians say Montjoy came the next day, and his statement was by that time a formality. The play sums up Henry's view: "God fought for us," and he orders "be it death proclaimed throughout our host to boast of this, or take that praise from God which is his only." The Psalm Henry V directed his men to sing on the field, "Non nobis, Domine," says, "[N]ot to us, God, but to your name the glory."

Not only had the outnumbered English won an unexpected victory, but the cost to the French was astounding. The dead included much of the leadership of the country: the Constable of France; the dukes of Alencon, Brabant, and Bar; and a huge number of the French nobility (according to Holinshed more than one hundred twenty princes and nobles were among the ten thousand French dead, while the dukes of Orleans and Bourbon were among the prisoners). Yet, English losses were minimal – besides the duke of York, the earl of Suffolk, and a few other men of note, "five or six hundred persons."

The Final Act

The peace conference and Henry's scene with Princess Catherine are an abbreviated version of what was, in reality, a much longer process. Henry V completed his journey to Calais and returned to a tumultuous welcome in England. In 1417 CE, he invaded France again, this time with goal of capturing all of Normandy. In 1420 CE, after the French agreed to the Treaty of Troyes, he married Catherine, Charles VI's youngest daughter, and was proclaimed the Heir of France, meaning that the children of that marriage would inherit the crowns of both England and France. It was actually the second recent marriage between the royal houses of England and France: Henry V's predecessor Richard II had been married to Catherine's older sister, Isabel. However, they had no children, and in any case there had never been an agreement that their children would inherit the French crown. The Treaty of Troyes also specifically disinherited Charles VI's son.

Henry's clumsy attempts in the play to woo Catherine in broken French are charming and probably found a sympathetic audience in London circa 1600 CE. Yet it is highly unlikely that the historic Henry lacked an expert command of French. After all, Henry saw himself as the legitimate heir to the French throne. In the early 1400s, diplomatic exchanges between the parties in these years were in Latin or French, and upper-class English children learned French in their nurseries. But by Shakespeare's time, the relationship between France and England was a good deal more remote.

In theory, Henry's marriage to Catherine and the Treaty of Troyes successfully completed the process begun nearly a century before when Edward III of England had asserted that he was the rightful heir to the French crown. The son of Henry V and Catherine became – at least in title – king of both realms. But he was only a child. Charles VI of France and Henry V of England both died in 1422 CE, when Henry VI was less than a year old. The dauphin of France had never acceded to the Treaty of Troyes that disinherited him, and his cause was taken up by Joan of Arc. She helped spearhead the French opposition that led to Charles's coronation as king of France at Rheims in 1429 CE and the long French campaign to expel the English. Meanwhile, England's divided government under the nominal leadership of a child king failed to establish a firm grasp on Henry V's territorial gains.

Chorus sums it up this way in the final words of the play: "Henry the Sixth, in infant bands crowned king of France and England, did this king succeed; whose state so many had the managing, that they lost France and made his England bleed." (Chorus also adds "which oft our stage hath shown" because Shakespeare's *Henry VI* plays, while following *Henry V* in historical order, were produced first.)

For Further Viewing

There are two excellent – but very different – filmed versions of Shakespeare's *Henry V*. The first, directed by and starring Laurence Olivier, was made in 1944 during World War II as a morale booster for British troops and civilians. As might be expected, it emphasizes the noble side of Henry and leaves out elements such as the plot to kill him and Henry's threats to the citizens of Harfleur. It opens on a reproduction of Shakespeare's Globe Theater, where the camera follows the actors on- and backstage, before moving to more cinematic exteriors. The

German army was then occupying northern France, so shooting on historic locations was impossible, and it was decided that even English exteriors were a poor choice, given possible overflights by both Allied and enemy aircraft. Therefore, the climactic battle scene was filmed in neutral Ireland. Olivier was a stage rather than a movie actor at heart, but his talent and insight into the character make the film memorable.

Kenneth Branagh's 1989 film version is less stagey and a good deal darker, but just as compelling. More intimate than Olivier's, it effectively uses light and shadow to illuminate the characters' psyches, particularly Henry's. In addition, the 1944 version makes the French seem largely inept and plays on Charles VI's mental illness to make him seem particularly ill-suited to kingship (ironic since during the war the French were allies of the English). In Branagh's version, Paul Scofield plays the king of France as a troubled but moving character. The battle scenes are also a harsh and convincing portrait of a muddy, confused, and brutal conflict.

7

"Once more we sit in England's royal throne"

Henry VI

The *Henry VI* trilogy, sometimes known as "the contention plays," is about a half-century contest for power among the noble ranks of England. There are occasional conflicts over ideology or policy – how to prosecute the war in France, for instance. But, by and large, the dispute is over which group of cousins is to rule the country – a dispute that effectively began at the end of the reign of King Richard II, when his cousin Henry Bolingbroke deposed Richard and made himself King Henry IV.

Many of the key players in the *Henry VI* dramas, particularly *Part 1*, were alive in 1400 CE when that deposition occurred. After the deposition, Henry IV had managed – barely – to keep his crown despite rebellions all over England during most of his thirteen-year reign. His son, Henry V, had quieted dissent by taking the conflict to France and winning decisive victories at Agincourt and in Normandy that legitimized his kingship. But when Henry V's death left the country with an infant as his successor, the underlying divisions broke out into the open again. *Henry VI, Part 1* is largely concerned with how those divisions affected the English attempt to retain Henry V's conquests in France. *Part 2* and *Part 3* cover the later years, when the conflict focused on England.

The unifying figure in all the plays is Henry VI, whose reign lasted almost fifty years. Henry was born in 1421 CE at Windsor while his father was campaigning in France, consolidating the victories he had won at Agincourt in 1415 CE and later in Normandy. Among the fruits of those victories, as noted, had been the hand of Catherine, the daughter of the French king, Charles VI, and the promise that the son of Henry and Catherine would inherit not only the crown of England but also the crown of France. Those inheritances came into effect not long after Henry VI's birth. His father, Henry V, died of disease while campaigning in France in 1422 CE, followed shortly thereafter by his grandfather Charles VI, making Henry VI, at least in theory, the ruler of both kingdoms.

Henry VI may have reigned from 1422 to 1471 CE, but for long periods he didn't really rule. Because he became king before his first birthday, during his early years management of the kingdom was unhappily divided between a council of state and his uncle, the duke of Gloucester. In his mature years, Henry was unable to assert any real control over the warring factions of the kingdom, in part because he was troubled, like his grandfather Charles VI of France, by periods of mental illness. Then, for the better part of a decade, Henry VI was in hiding or in prison, before being briefly restored to the throne.

This period marked the end of Hundred Years' War with France. The internecine conflict that overlapped and followed is now known as the Wars of the Roses. Neither term was in use during the period, though Shakespeare invents a scene where the factions choose a red rose and white to identify themselves. In reality, they used a variety of signs and battlefield devices, but not roses.

The Rightful King

Primogeniture – inheritance by the oldest son – promises the virtue of simplicity and predictability, but in practice it has a number of shortcomings, particularly in the political sphere. What if the oldest son has a son of his own, then dies, while the dead king has a brother who is still alive? This was the issue in *King John*; he was the brother of the late king who was disputing the crown with the son of another brother. What if the eldest son of the deceased king is unable to exercise the key duties of a medieval monarch – to lead his country in war and to produce an heir? This – in addition to general mismanagement – was the problem with Richard II, who preferred diplomacy to war and who was apparently incapable of fathering an heir. What if there were no direct heir through the male line – king to first son to first son – but there was a male heir through the female line – king to daughter to son? The French interpreted their law to make inheritance through the female line impossible, a position disputed by England's King

Edward III, who started the Hundred Years' War to assert his claim to the open French throne as the son of the deceased French king's sister. On the other hand, does the first son of someone who got to the throne by irregular means – say, by a coup – automatically have a clear claim to the crown? What about his son, in turn? In the *Henry VI* plays, this question is the crux of the eventual dispute.

Like most ruling oligarchies, the noble class of England married largely within itself or – in the case of the royal family – within the ranks of the noble families of Europe, producing ever-more complex family trees. By the second generation, lines of descent were complicated; by the third, they could be impossibly tangled. Yet the issue was not academic. All the major English contestants for the throne in these plays trace their lineage back to King Edward III and his sons, most through the third surviving son, John of Gaunt – he was the duke of Lancaster, and that name became attached to the party of his descendants. But there is a whole line that goes back to Edward III's second surviving son, Lionel, and eventually through the Mortimer family. For a variety of reasons, the claims of this line had been ignored or suppressed. But by the time of Henry VI, the representative of this line of inheritance was the duke of York.

There was nothing overwhelmingly compelling about most competing claims, and every royal house in Europe included relatives who could make a case that they, rather than the current monarch, should have inherited the crown. During a generally successful kingship, such claims were usually kept private. Given that the penalty for an unsuccessful attempt to assert them was a very painful death, most claimants opted for discretion.

The Hundred Years' War

The three *Henry VI* plays cover the period in which the Hundred Years' War came to an end. While the conflict had spanned decades, fighting was intermittent and, for long periods was dormant. It is frequently interpreted as a battle between the English and French, but it was just as much a civil war inside France. Divisions among the French proved vital to England's success. By Henry V's reign, nobles such as the duke of Burgundy and the duke of Britanny controlled huge swaths of territory, had substantial armies of their own, and were fighting to control the French crown. Henry V's military successes in France – including the victory at Agincourt (see *Henry V*) – owed a great deal to the fact that the duke of Burgundy, who controlled much of northern France and what would become the Low Countries, was either actively allied with Henry or remained neutral.

A divided France was critical if the English were to retain the territories won by Henry V. Medieval governments simply did not have the economic resources necessary to sustain a lengthy war or even a long occupation. When the French were divided and unable to mount an aggressive counteroffensive, the English could maintain their holdings, but once the

French united – as they eventually do in these plays – the English military situation became unsustainable.

Joan of Arc

The uniting of the French came about under the dauphin, a son of Charles VI who had been disinherited in the Treaty of Troyes that promised the crown of France to the son of Henry V and the dauphin's sister, Catherine. A key factor in his renaissance was Joan of Arc. Joan was a peasant girl who believed that God had given her the mission of driving the English out of France. She talked her way into the service of the dauphin, inspired and sometimes led his troops to important early victories, and was instrumental in his eventual crowning in Rheims, a challenge to the English assertion that Henry VI was the lawful king of France. Joan was canonized by the Roman Catholic Church and is a French national hero. She has been the subject of books, plays, and movies, almost all adulatory; but the English of Shakespeare's time considered her a villain, a witch whose military success against the English was due to her pact with the devil.

The Wars of the Roses

The long twilight of English power in France had much to do with the French making common cause against the invader, but it was also related to the huge vacuum at the center of English political life, a vacuum that opened up when Henry V died. Henry's death-bed wish had put his son's older uncle, the duke of

Bedford, in charge of the military situation in France while his younger uncle, the duke of Gloucester, was made Protector of the Realm. Whatever the military pressure that inspired Henry to make this choice, Bedford was not about to allow his younger brother effectively to assume the mantle of power in England. In this resolve he was joined by the royal council, which was determined to assert itself and manage the kingdom until young Henry VI came of age.

Jack Cade's Rebellion

Late in Henry VI's reign, in the spring of 1450 CE, thousands of peasants, small merchants, and landholders from Kent in the southeast of England, led by Jack Cade, marched on the capitol to protest King Henry's government. Their petition, "The Complaint of the Poor Commons of Kent," attacked "the insatiable, covetous, malicious persons" around the king. Thanks to their mismanagement, the petition said, "his merchandise is lost, his common people is destroyed, the sea is lost, France is lost, the King himself . . . owes more than ever any King of England ought." The rebels executed some royal officials, began plundering London, and were eventually bested during a long battle at London Bridge. They dispersed after the Lord Chamberlain issued official pardons. Cade was killed in a later skirmish and thirty-four other rebel leaders were ultimately executed.

The "Complaint" specifically states, "We will that all men know that we blame not all the Lords, nor all those that are about the King's person . . . nor all men of law . . . ," but one of Cade's followers in

Shakespeare's play, Dick the Butcher, utters the line that has resonated down the ages: "[T]he first thing we do, let's kill all the lawyers."

The Factions and the Lancaster Line

In *Henry VI, Part 1*, the leaders of the factions are basically all Lancasters, as was Henry V. Henry V's brothers – the dukes of Gloucester and Bedford – shared that lineage with his son, Henry VI. All of them descended from the marriage of John of Gaunt to Blanche of Lancaster. But then it gets complicated. Gaunt was married twice more, and the descendants of his marriage to his third wife, Catherine Swynford, became known as the Beauforts. The Beaufort line was at first illegitimate because the children were born when the lady in question was Gaunt's mistress rather than his wife, but they were legitimized after Gaunt's second wife died and he married Catherine. The Beauforts had a power base of their own, and in the first play Somerset, Exeter, and the bishop of Winchester are all Beauforts.

By the later plays, the Lancaster faction is led by Henry VI's wife, Margaret of Anjou, while her husband is either imprisoned or otherwise incapable of leadership. Although the Lancastrians retain some internal tensions, their conflicts have become secondary to their overall battle with the Yorkists, led by the duke of York and his adherents. Membership of the factions constantly shifts, as some nobles are active or inactive at a particular time, or – as in the case of Warwick and even the brother of the duke of York – switch sides.

Alarums and Excursions

The *Henry VI* histories are among the early plays of Shakespeare and, to a certain extent, can be described as "action movies" for the Elizabethan stage. For instance, *Part 1* has repeated "alarums and excursions," groups of men in armor sweeping across the stage in mock battles or pretend sieges of castles or towns in the play the English successfully repel a French attack on Orleans, lose the city to a second French assault, and in a third incident win the city back. The adherents of the bishop of Winchester and of Gloucester engage in two major brawls, one before both the Tower of London and the other outside parliament. Joan of Arc fights duels with both the dauphin and the English leader John Talbot. *Part 2* includes a long series of scenes of fighting and the extensive depredations of Jack Cade's uprising, while *Part 3* has further battles and dramatic confrontations.

The Principal Players

The three plays span decades and tell a complicated story with dozens of characters. But the most important are as follows:

King Henry VI, at his best, not much of a king; at his worst, so troubled by mental illness that he could not function
Duke of Gloucester, Henry's uncle, Protector of the Realm

Duke of Bedford, another uncle, older than Gloucester, left by Henry V to hold France but unwilling to let his younger brother, Gloucester, control the throne

Bishop (later Cardinal) of Winchester, a member of the Beaufort family related to the royal house and closely associated with the royal council; an adversary of Gloucester in terms of who would rule England

Duke of Exeter, ally of the bishop of Winchester

Duke of Somerset, a Lancastrian

Margaret of Anjou, French bride of Henry VI, and eventual center of the Lancaster faction

Duke of Suffolk, an ally (and in the play a lover) of Queen Margaret

Richard, Duke of York, the eventual claimant of the Crown

Edward, George, and Richard, his sons, leaders of the Yorkist faction in the Wars of the Roses

Duke of Warwick, the richest man in England, leading ally of the Yorkists (for most of the play)

Part 1

Henry VI, Part 1, begins over Henry V's coffin, and the occasion soon degenerates into a dispute between Gloucester and the bishop of Winchester. Their quarrel is interrupted by three different messengers, who bring news of England's losses in France and the crowning of the dauphin (in reality, these events were spread out over years). The scene then shifts to France and the arrival of Joan La Pucelle. (The details of Joan of Arc's meeting with the dauphin are taken from Holinshed, though not the duel the dauphin uses to test her mettle.) Although her English opponents treat her with scorn, Shakespeare has given her some wonderful lines, including, "assigned am I to be the English scourge" and "fight to the last gasp."

Back in England, Shakespeare dramatizes the riot at the Tower of London between Gloucester and his men and the bishop of Winchester and his adherents. The bishop accuses Gloucester of wanting to enter the Tower to get arms so he can take control of the Crown, and the brawl stands as an example of what Holinshed says of their conflict: "the whole realm was troubled with them and their partakers."

Moving back to France again, the play tells the story of the death of the earl of Salisbury, killed by a cannon shot as he looked over the defenses of Orleans. It is lifted from Holinshed, including the fact that the fatal shot was fired by a child, the son of the gunner. The father, says Holinshed, was not at his post because he "was gone down to dinner." The garden scene – a Shakespearean creation – lays out the red rose/white rose conflict between Lancaster (represented by Somerset) and York. One of the issues discussed is the fact that York's father was executed for treason by Henry V.

In the following scene, Shakespeare recapitulates the dynastic dispute for the audience. Edmund Mortimer explains that the duke of York's father was executed for plotting to put him (Mortimer) on the throne, and Mortimer goes over the justice of his family's claim of descent from Edward III's second son. That claim to the throne now rests on the York who sits before him, as he is Mortimer's nephew, and Mortimer himself is dying. (The real Edmund Mortimer warned Henry V of the plot against him, was held harmless by Henry, and joined in the campaign in France, eventually dying in Ireland in 1425 CE. His estate, however, did pass to Richard, later duke of York.)

Despite the potential legitimacy of York's claim, the play shows Henry VI restoring York at last to his dead father's estates, and he is made the chief English leader in France. Shakespeare balances the continuing court disputes with repeated scenes of English heroism in France. In the next sequence, the brave English war leader John Talbot dies in battle, joined by his young son, who refuses to leave his side; Talbot's defeat is shown to be in part a result of quarreling between York and Somerset over who was to reinforce him.

As the play indicates, negotiations were underway to marry Henry VI to the daughter of the duke of Armagnac, a major power in France, when the duke of Suffolk persuaded the king to marry instead Margaret of Anjou. She was the daughter of the duke of Anjou, who also claimed the titles of king of Sicily and of Jerusalem, though as Gloucester notes, "Her father is no better than an earl, though in glorious titles he excel." (Although she was a figure at the French court and related to the king, her relative impoverishment proved to be a major factor in English reaction to the match. The play also depicts her as Suffolk's prisoner, which she never was.)

Joan of Arc had been portrayed as a brave opponent, but the play now begins to show another side of her character. Her downfall begins when she calls forth the spirits of the underworld, offering her body and soul if they will help her defeat the English. After being captured by the duke of York, she asserts that she is of noble birth (rejecting her shepherd father, whom the English have brought to her trial). She first claims to be a virgin, then to be pregnant (pregnant women were not supposed to face capital punishment). However, she is sent off to execution by York, who says, "[S]trumpet, thy words condemn thy brat and thee." Joan actually was captured by French opponents of the dauphin and handed over to the English. She was tried and executed as a heretic, though her name was later cleared of the charge of heresy by a church investigation, and she eventually was canonized.

The play closes with Suffolk boasting to the audience of his success in getting Henry to assent to the marriage with Margaret, who "shall now be queen, and rule the king but I will rule her, the king, and realm."

In addition to combining events and embroidering the story of Joan of Arc, Shakespeare takes many other liberties with the actual history. To name two, *Part 1* shows Henry VI crowned in Paris as a grown man (in fact it happened in 1431 CE, when he was ten) and Joan of Arc convincing the duke of Burgundy to switch sides from the English to the French (which happened after her death).

Part 2

This play is a portrait of the destructive effects of ambition, with virtually no truly sympathetic character other than Duke Humphrey of Gloucester,

Lord Protector of the Realm. The king himself is not a participant in the conspiracies; Shakespeare's characterization of him matches the chronicler Edward Hall's description: "a man of a meek spirit and of a simple wit, preferring peace before war, rest before business, honesty before profit and quietness before labor. . . ." But virtually everyone else in the royal circle has Gloucester in his sights.

The drama opens with the arrival of Margaret of Anjou, the queen-to-be, and the revelation of the treaty that brought her to England. She has come not only without a dowry but also at the cost of the French districts of Maine and Anjou, the territories that constitute "the keys of Normandy" then held by the English and traded away as part of the marriage compact with the French king. "Shameful is this league, fatal is this marriage," says Gloucester, and everybody turns on Suffolk, who made the deal and brought Margaret to England. (Most historians believe giving up Maine and Anjou was the king's idea, not Suffolk's, as part of Henry's long-term attempt to reach an accommodation with France.)

Many of the major characters want to see Gloucester brought low, from Cardinal Beaufort to Somerset to Buckingham, but all because of their own ambition, especially Beaufort, who hopes to replace him as Lord Protector. Yet, none trusts the others enough to mount an effective conspiracy. When the others have left the stage, the duke of York announces to the audience that his ambition goes past replacing Gloucester: "The day will come when York shall claim his own . . . and when I spy advantage claim the throne."

The only person who seems immune to ambition is Gloucester, but the next scene shows that his wife has enough for both of them. "Are not thou second woman in the realm?" Gloucester asks his duchess, begging her to abandon her desire to be queen. (Because Gloucester was a brother of Henry V, he would have been a candidate for the crown if Henry VI were to die without an heir.) But the Duchess's highborn manners have put off a number of people at court, not the least Queen Margaret. "Strangers in court do take her for the queen," the real queen remarks.

Sorcery was widely believed effective both in the time of Henry VI and of Shakespeare, and the séance scene involving the Duchess offered a great opportunity for eerie stagecraft and audience-pleasing special effects. In real life the Duchess was arrested for consorting with witches, though Hall's account, which says that the witch and her collaborators "had devised an image of wax representing the King, which by their sorcery a little and little consumed, intending thereby in conclusion to waste and destroy the King's person, and so bring him to death," was a good deal less dramatic than the scene that appears in the play.

Most of those involved in the witchcraft episode were executed. The Duchess, in view of her rank, was allowed to live, though she was publicly humiliated and banished to the Isle of Man. In the play, Gloucester, knowing his public responsibilities, refuses to intercede for her, but tells her jailer, "Use her well; the world may laugh again, and I may live to do you kindness if you do it her." Queen Margaret's role in the downfall of the Duchess is Shakespeare's creation. Eleanor was tried and convicted in 1441 CE; Margaret of Anjou was then twelve years old, and would not arrive in England for another three years.

The conviction of Gloucester's wife marks the beginning of his own downfall. The conspirators, led by the Queen, contrive to bring him before a parliamentary trial for a list of offenses, many of which are imagined. Although a number of the conspirators are willing to take on the task, it is Suffolk who hires the murderers to dispose of Gloucester, and it is he who breaks the news of Gloucester's death. When Warwick arrives, he comes to the obvious conclusion, based on Gloucester's bulging eyes and blackened face: "[V]iolent hands were laid upon the life of this thrice-famed Duke." According to Hall, "all indifferent persons well knew that he died no natural death, but of some violent force." But to the extent that modern historians can determine from reports of Gloucester's death, the evidence could also point to a stroke.

Gloucester's death is laid at the feet of Suffolk, and he is banished by the king, under pressure from the Commons and his opponents at court. His departure from Queen Margaret is a moving testament to their affection (particularly coming from two people who have just collaborated in the murder of the play's most admirable character). "For where thou art, there is the world itself . . . and where not, desolation," Suffolk tells her. It was rumored at the time – and since – that they were lovers, although they were decades apart in age and there is no real evidence to justify such a charge.

On his way into exile, Suffolk, in disguise, is captured by pirates. He loudly proclaims his station, but the pirates, it appears, are patriotic if not law-abiding, and execute him for his role in mismanaging the realm. "By devilish policy art thou grown great," the pirate leader tells him, and Suffolk meets his death protesting, "It is impossible that I should die by such a lowly vassal as thyself." (According to Holinshed, the ship that intercepted his was not a pirate ship, but one owned by the duke of Exeter.)

Shortly thereafter, Cardinal Beaufort meets his end, apparently by natural causes. On his deathbed, the Cardinal raves, promising to give "England's treasure, enough to purchase such another island," if death will pass him by and saying, obviously of Gloucester, "Died he not in bed? . . . O torture me no more! I will confess." Says Warwick, "So bad a death argues a monstrous life." Holinshed reports that Beaufort on his deathbed told his confessor that seeing the deaths of his nephews, first Bedford, then Gloucester, "I thought myself equal with kings" and added, "why should I die, having so much riches . . . but I see now that the world faileth me."

A Touch of Class

The groundlings were the audience members who paid a penny to stand before the stage in Elizabethan theaters (the seats – more expensive – were in the galleries around the standing area). Most Shakespeare histories include some scenes or characters with whom the groundlings could identify; such scenes are often humorous, with characters speaking in dialect or working-class accents. *Part 2* includes several such scenes, as well as an extended sequence with an aggressively working-class cast – the participants in Jack Cade's Rebellion.

In one early scene, an armorer and his apprentice fight to determine the truth of the apprentice's accusation that his master said the duke of York was the rightful king (a treasonous remark); in another, a man who claims to have been cured of blindness by a miracle is revealed to be an imposter. (The stories are lifted from Hall's *Union of Two Noble and Illustrious Families* and John Foxe's *Book of Martyrs*.)

Almost all of act 4 is concerned with Cade's rebellion, which begins with an attack on a schoolmaster because he can read and write. "Dost thou used to write thy name, or hast thou a mark to thyself, like an honest, plain-dealing man?" asks Cade. When the man confesses that he can indeed write his name, Cade has him hauled away, saying "Hang him with his pen and inkhorn around his neck." In the play, as in history, Cade's forces defeat troops led by Sir Humphrey Stafford and eventually invade London. Cade's followers executed some royal officials but were eventually persuaded to disperse.

One of the features of Cade's Rebellion was its link to York and the Mortimers. Cade sometimes used the name of Mortimer, and in the play he claims his father was the son of Edmund Mortimer and a daughter of Lionel, the duke of Clarence. According to Cade, as a child his father was "by a beggar-woman stol'n away, and, ignorant of his birth and parentage, became a bricklayer when he came of age."

Shakespeare implies York's involvement from a distance in Cade's Rebellion, a claim that not all historians support. Whatever York's role, he did eventually return from his post in Ireland, enraged at the mismanagement of England and at further losses in France, which he blamed on Somerset. Persuaded in the play that Somerset has been arrested, he momentarily relents until he discovers that Somerset is actually at liberty. York then openly challenges the king as "not fit to govern and rule multitudes." The final scenes of the play dramatize the first Battle of St. Alban's, in which York, assisted by Warwick, is triumphant. But their victory is not complete because the king and queen survive and flee to safety in London.

It is in the last part of this play that Richard, York's son, begins to emerge as a character and a strong supporter of his father's cause. In the play, he kills Somerset (who died in the battle, but it is not clear at whose hands).

Anomalies

Close readers will note that in *Part 1*, Henry is crowned in France as an adult, and at the end of the play he talks of a special tax – a tenth – that has to be raised to bring his future queen from France in appropriate style. Yet a few scenes later, in the opening of *Part 2*, Gloucester speaks of how the English "had his highness in his infancy crowned in Paris," and he criticizes Suffolk for demanding "a whole fifteenth for costs and charges in transporting" the queen-to-be.

Part 3

The final drama in the trilogy takes the story through York's rebellion and the eventual triumph of his oldest son, Edward, crowned Edward IV. The play compresses years of intermittent struggle, during which the effective rule of England switched back and forth between Lancaster and York until the Yorkists' final victory. In *Part 3*, the Yorkists, having won the battle at St. Albans that closes *Part 2*, lose the Battle of Wakefield, win the Battle of Towton, lose a conflict in which Edward is captured by his former ally Warwick, win the Battle of Barnet (in which Edward is joined by his brother, who at one point had switched sides to join Warwick), and finally triumph at the Battle of Tewkesbury.

The play gives little sense of the actual timelines of events. In fact, the first Battle of St. Albans, which closes *Part 2,* was in 1455 CE, while the Battle of Tewkesbury took place sixteen years later, in 1471 CE; there were also other significant battles that the play does not mention.

Part 3 begins with the duke of York and his sons and allies, fresh from their victory at the first St. Albans conflict, arriving in London to seize power. York literally takes the throne and is sitting on it when Henry VI enters. "Thou factious duke of York, descend my throne," says Henry, but York refuses, agreeing only after Henry suggests that York become his heir. Henry's remaining allies, Lords Clifford, Westmoreland, and Northumberland, leave in disgust. "Farewell faint-hearted and degenerate king," says Westmoreland.

Queen Margaret, informed that her son has been disinherited, makes the loudest objections. "Thou timorous wretch," she tells the king, "thou preferr'st thy life before thine honor." She departs, son Prince Edward in tow, to raise an army among the northern lords to reverse the decision. (Hall says York decided not to seize the crown directly but to leave Henry in place so as not to "stir and provoke the fury and ire of the common people.")

Later, York is persuaded by his sons not to wait for Henry's death to claim the crown, and the following scenes from the Battle of Wakefield illustrate the level of bitterness of the conflict. Clifford, on the king's side, kills the duke of York's unarmed son, a schoolboy, in revenge for the death of Clifford's father's at York's hands in the previous play (the young man in question, the earl of Rutland, was actually seventeen and thus of military age by medieval standards). When the duke of York is captured by the Lancastrian forces, the queen mocks him and shows him a napkin stained with his son's blood. "O tiger's heart wrapped in a woman's hide," says York, before he is executed and his head set atop the gates of the city, "so York may overlook the town of York," in the words of the queen.

The Yorkists are down but not out. Warwick escapes a later defeat by the queen's forces and joins York's sons George, Richard, and Edward, as the dead duke's oldest son now proclaims himself the new duke of York. The Yorkists then meet the Lancastrians at Towton, fortune this time swinging to the Yorkist side. Clifford is killed in the battle, and the Yorkists replace their father's head on the city's battlements with Clifford's.

The Yorkist victory at Towton has placed the new duke of York on the throne as King Edward IV. The Lancastrians disperse: the Queen and her son to France to seek a new alliance, and Henry, we later learn, to Scotland. He is captured in a forest in England by two gamekeepers who recognize him after he has come back "to greet mine own land with my wishful sight." (He was actually captured at a sympathizer's house in the north of England.) King Edward IV falls prey to the charms of the widow Lady Elizabeth Gray, who has come to him to petition that her lands be returned to her, lands which were taken away because her late husband had fought on the Lancaster side. (Edward IV had a reputation as a ladies' man – "the wanton Edward" Queen Margaret calls him – a characteristic he shared with his grandson Henry VIII.)

However romantic the match, it is politically inconvenient. Warwick has been in France negotiating on King Edward's behalf for the hand of the French king's daughter. Margaret is also at the French court seeking aid for her cause, but the French are clearly leaning to the sitting King Edward rather than the deposed King Henry. However, the situation changes when word is brought that Edward has married Elizabeth Gray. Says Hall, "The French King and his Queen were not a little discontent (as I cannot blame them) to have their sister first demanded and then granted, and in conclusion rejected."

An insulted Warwick switches sides, saying of Edward, "I here renounce him and return to Henry" and telling Queen Margaret, "henceforth I am thy true servitor." He says of his former ally King Edward, "I was the chief that raised him to the crown, and I'll be chief to bring him down again." To confirm his new loyalties, Warwick promises to marry his daughter to Prince Edward, the son of King Henry and Queen Margaret. On the news that Warwick and the queen have joined forces, King Edward's younger brother, George, duke of Clarence, abandons his brother to join Warwick (he married Warwick's other daughter). Richard, however, stays with Edward, adding in an aside, "Not for love of Edward, but the crown."

Fortunes change again. Warwick and his new allies the Lancastrians capture King Edward in Warwickshire. He is imprisoned while Warwick returns to London and recrowns King Henry, who resigns the actual government to Warwick and the duke of Clarence "while I myself will lead a private life, and in devotion spend my latter days."

But wait – it's not over yet.

Richard frees Edward from his imprisonment in the north of England (not a difficult task in the play because Edward was allowed to go out hunting every day), and Edward heads for the Continent to raise a new army. He returns to England at the head of his troops, captures King Henry, and sends him to the Tower, then leaves to give battle to his former ally Warwick and the remaining Lancastrian forces.

At Coventry, the Lancastrians are now gathering, led by Warwick. The duke of Clarence shows up with his own forces, but instead of joining his new allies in the city, he switches sides again and rejoins his brother King Edward. In the following battle at nearby Barnet, Edward and the Yorkists win, while Warwick is killed. The queen is then defeated at the head of a force of French at the Battle of Tewkesbury.

Some historians say that the young prince died on the battlefield, while others, including Hall, state that he was executed afterward (but not before his mother's eyes, as in the play). To cap the Yorkist triumph, Richard hastens to the Tower of London, where he kills King Henry. (The historical Henry did die in the Tower, and contemporaries believed it was at Richard's hands, or at least in Richard's presence and by his orders.)

Edward opens the last scene with the words, "Once more we sit in England's royal throne, repurchased with the blood of enemies," and he rejoices in having "my country's peace and brothers' loves."

Afterthoughts

In the *Henry VI* plays, it is clear that part of the blame for the continuing struggle is a simple clash of egos, along with a desire for revenge. Edward says to Margaret, "But what hath broached this tumult but thy pride? Had'st thou been meek, our title still had slept," while the dying Clifford lays the responsibility on Henry VI, for whom he has fought: "Had thou swayed as kings should do . . . thou this day had kept thy chair in peace . . . what makes robbers bold but too much lenity?" At the same time, Shakespeare makes clear the human cost of civil war in a scene where a father has killed his son, fighting on the opposite side, and a son discovers that he has similarly killed his father.

Although few of the major characters in *Part 3* are particularly admirable, the play goes to great length to cast Richard in a negative light. His physical deformity is referred to repeatedly: The queen calls him a "crookback prodigy" and "a foul misshapen stigmatic." In asides and soliloquies he tells the audience of his plots and conspiracies to become king. As part of his struggle to "torment myself to catch the English crown," he can "smile, and murder whiles I smile . . . and wet my cheeks with artificial tears . . . and set the murderous Machaivel to school." (His mention of Machiavelli is an anomaly; *The Prince* was not published until decades after Richard's death.) After murdering King Henry, he says, "Clarence, thy turn is next, and then the rest" of those who stand between him and the throne, a prophecy that will be fulfilled in *Richard III*.

For Further Viewing

Given the scope of the trilogy and its relatively large cast (who can keep track of Suffolk, Somerset, Salisbury, Stafford, and Stanley, not to mention two dukes of Gloucester, two dukes of York, and any number of Beauforts?), the best introduction may be to watch the 1983 BBC television version, produced by Jonathan Miller and directed by Jane Howell. Notable performances include Trevor Peacock as both Lord Talbot and Jack Cade, Brenda Blethlyn as Joan of Arc, David Burke as the duke of Gloucester (*Parts 1* and *2*), and Julia Foster as Queen Margaret. Many public libraries have the entire BBC series on video.

8

"Full of danger is the Duke of Gloucester"

Richard III

This is the last of the connected plays of
Shakespeare's history cycle, and in many ways it
is a direct sequel to *Henry VI, Part 3*. The *Henry
VI* plays dramatized the long period when he was
king of England, although to say that he actually ruled
during much of that time would be an overstatement.
Henry's mental instability, combined with the English
military being overextended in France, led to the loss
of most of England's French possessions; both issues
contributed to the long internecine English conflict,
as noted, later known as the Wars of the Roses. This
was a series of battles between the Lancasters – Henry
VI, his queen, Margaret, and their allies – and the
duke of York and his allies, who claimed York had
a better claim to the English crown than Henry did.
After a series of reversals of fortune (see *Henry VI*)
the Yorkists won, placing Edward IV on the throne
and leaving Edward's brothers, George, the duke of

Clarence, and Richard, the duke of Gloucester, in positions of authority.

The drama opens only a few years after the death of Henry VI. Many of the principal characters carry over from the previous plays, including Richard himself; his brothers, King Edward IV and the duke of Clarence; old Queen Margaret (although her role is often omitted in modern stagings); Lady Anne, widow of Prince Edward, the son and heir of Henry VI who was killed in the Wars of Roses; and even King Henry VI himself, albeit only as a corpse. The central struggle remains the same as in the three parts of *Henry VI* – who will control the throne and establish a successful dynasty? But the structure and tone of the plays are quite different. The *Henry VI* plays tell a wide-ranging story involving dozens of characters, of whom King Henry is far from the most important. *Richard III*, however, is about one man and the lengths to which he will go to acquire and maintain power. The previous plays engage the audience as an audience, watching events occur and sometimes listening in when a character, as part of a prayer or a public conversation with himself, talks about his state of mind or his plans. *Richard III*, however, is full not only of such soliloquies, but also of asides, communications directly with the audience that comment upon events or characters or warn the onlookers of what is to come next.

Edward IV and Elizabeth Woodville

In the previous play, Edward IV had become enamored of Elizabeth Gray (her family were the Woodvilles), a widow whose husband had died fighting for the opposite side – the Lancasters – in the civil wars. The fact that he had married her enraged some of his allies, particularly the powerful duke of Warwick, who was trying to arrange for Edward a diplomatic marriage in France. (Warwick changed sides as a result.) Edward was confirmed on the throne by the final Yorkist victory at Tewkesbury, but internal dissension continued.

Many of King Edward's allies – including his brother, the duke of Clarence – were angry at the king for the preferment he ended up showing to the queen's family, arranging favorable marriages for them and giving them important and lucrative offices. By the time of the play, the Woodvilles – the queen, Earl Rivers, the Marquess of Dorset, and Lord Grey – have put together a powerful faction at court.

Richard's Deformity

The *Henry VI* plays made it clear that Richard had some sort of deformity – as seen, Queen Margaret called him a "crookback prodigy." Sir Thomas More's history of the period describes him as "little of stature, ill-featured of limbs . . . his left shoulder much higher than his right." Richard describes himself in his opening soliloquy of this play as having come into the world "but half-made up, and that so lamely and unfashionable that dogs bark at me. . . ." He is played as a hunchback in many modern stagings, but how prominent his actual deformity was remains open to question. His official portrait does not reflect it, although it would not be the first such portrait to be "painted up" to make the sitter more attractive. It does not seem to have kept him from being a successful military man, and even his enemies concede him to have been an effective soldier and leader.

In the Tudor version of history, reflected in Shakespeare's sources, Richard's physical deformity was an indication of, and a metaphor for, his moral failings. The Tudors, of course, had every reason to call into question the reputation of the man they killed and replaced on the throne. Many later writers believe that whereas Richard was certainly no moral paragon, his evil nature may have been overstated by the Tudors, and it is possible his physical problems were similarly overblown.

The Rise of Henry Tudor

In the earlier plays, the contenders for the throne were identified as adherents of either Lancaster or York. The Lancasters traced their descent from John of Gaunt, duke of Lancaster and father of Henry IV; the Yorkists came from an older brother of John of Gaunt, a line that ended up being identified with the Mortimer family, which had married into the family of the duke of York. The Tudors appear nowhere in this lineup. Who are they?

The answer may be found back in the time of Henry V. Henry V married Catherine, daughter of the French King Charles VI; their son was Henry VI, king (at least in title) of both England and France. Henry V died before his son was even a year old, so Henry VI was technically king from his infancy. It was the custom at the time that royal children were brought up away from the court and their parents, so Henry VI was soon adopted into a royal nursery and his youth was overseen by tutors picked by his uncles (who in the meantime were quarreling incessantly over who was to run the kingdom. See *Henry VI*). Thus, there was very little of a role for the now-dowager Queen Catherine, who was only in her twenties and had not been in England long enough to develop a following of her own. Her father had died shortly after her husband, and her surviving brother was contesting the French crown with her infant son. With no one particularly interested in her, she was shunted aside and all but forgotten.

It is no surprise that she would find solace elsewhere, and in this case it was in the arms of a young Welsh gentleman of her household, Owen Tudor. They had four children, including Edmund Tudor. Catherine died in 1437 CE, and while there was some question about the orthodoxy of Catherine's marriage to Tudor (or if they were married at all in terms of English law), Henry VI recognized his half-siblings, making Edmund Tudor the earl of Richmond. Edmund Tudor married into the Beaufort family, another branch of the Lancasters (see *Henry IV* and *Henry VI* for further discussion of the Beauforts), and had a son named Henry Tudor. As a Lancaster, Henry Tudor fled England when the Yorkists took power, ending up in Brittany for more than a decade.

The Winter of Our Discontent

Richard sets the tone of his character and the play in the opening scene, where he lays out for the audience his plan to claw his way to power. If the audience needed any further proof of his character, it comes in the following scene, where he fondly greets his brother on his way to prison. We know the duke of Clarence to have been condemned by Richard's machinations, though both blame the queen, King Edward's wife.

The next scene, where Richard woos the Lady Anne, is in the play a testament to Richard's ability to dissemble and conceal his true nature, as he proceeds to seduce a woman whose husband and father-in-law he has killed, and to do so over her father-in-law's body. While Shakespeare has used the facts of the case to build this scene, he has also left out many facts.

Anne was the daughter of the duke of Warwick, and her marriage to Prince Edward, the son of Henry VI, was part of a political deal to bring Warwick, who had been the strongest supporter of the Yorkists, over to the Lancaster side. There was also some doubt as to whether the two were really married, or actually only pledged to each other, because Prince Edward's mother, the redoubtable Queen Margaret, may have discouraged her son from consummating the marriage. Anticipating the time when her son would be on the throne, the queen might well have been holding him out for a more diplomatic union. In any case, Richard and Anne would have probably known each other well, given the long alliance between her family and the Yorks.

The contest between the current queen's family and the king's relatives becomes clear in the first act, when Richard accuses Queen Elizabeth of working against the interests of his family, although she denies playing a role in having the duke of Clarence imprisoned. Queen Margaret, widow of Henry VI, makes an appearance here to comment on the action. The scene is Shakespeare's creation: Margaret was ransomed back to France in 1476 CE and died in 1482 CE. Her bitter recriminations – "Long mayst thou live to bewail thy children's death," she tells Elizabeth, her replacement as queen of England – recapitulate for the audience some of the events of the previous plays in the cycle.

The Death of the Duke of Clarence

Anne's father, the duke of Warwick, switched sides during the Wars of the Roses, abandoning his long association with the family of the duke of York to join with Queen Margaret and King Henry VI; other nobles did the same. But the most surprising switch had to be that of one of the Yorkist brothers, George, the duke of Clarence, who for a while joined Warwick on the Lancaster side. He switched back at the end of the war but continued to be a thorn in the side of his brother, King Edward IV, particularly because he felt that the king was favoring the queen's brothers and other relatives over his own family. As punishment for further attempts to foment rebellion, he was placed in the Tower and executed in 1478 after an order by parliament. Richard's role, if any, in this incident is unclear. Holinshed says that though King Edward consented to Clarence's death, "he much did both lament his infortunate chance and repent his sudden execution."

Other key characters in the drama include the duke of Buckingham and Lord Stanley, the earl of Derby. Buckingham had Lancastrian roots and had been reared in the household of the queen, who forced him to marry her much older sister, alienating him from the Woodville family. He took the side of Richard III after the death of Edward IV. Thomas Stanley, earl of Derby, was married first to a sister of the duke of Warwick, making him at least by association a Yorkist, and after her death to Margaret Beaufort, mother of the Lancastrian Henry Tudor, who opposed Richard III for the throne.

The death of King Edward IV in act 2 gets the plot moving. Arrangements are immediately made to send for the king's thirteen-year-old heir, Edward, the Prince of Wales, who is slated to become King Edward V. The issue now becomes which faction will have the most influence with the teenage monarch. Act 3, scene 2 reminds the audience of the dangers of a minority kingship – which had been disastrous for the country under Henry VI. As the citizens note, "full of danger is the duke of Gloucester," while the queen's sons and brothers are "haught and proud."

In the next scene, with the king-to-be on the road to London, news is brought to the queen that her brother and son have been arrested and taken to the north of England at the order of "the mighty dukes, Buckingham and Gloucester." Says the queen, "I see the ruin of my house," and she flees to sanctuary. "I want more uncles here to welcome me," says Prince Edward on his arrival, referring to the queen's brothers who have been arrested. "These uncles which you want were dangerous," replies Richard, who sends Edward to the Tower of London, allegedly for safekeeping, while others go off to get his younger brother, who is in sanctuary at Westminster Abbey with his mother and, as such, theoretically unreachable by civil law. There was a whole protocol around sanctuary in this period, but, as Buckingham says, "Oft have I heard of sanctuary men, but sanctuary children never till now."

With the princes on their way to the Tower, Richard's conspiracy to seize the throne moves into high gear. Buckingham sends Catesby to sound out the Lord Chamberlain, William Hastings, about his receptivity to a move by Richard for the crown. "Tell him," says Richard, "that his ancient knot of dangerous adversaries tomorrow are let blood at Pomfret Castle." (The Woodvilles were imprisoned there, and Hastings blamed them for his previous incarceration in the Tower.) The queen, says Holinshed, "[s]pecially grudged" Chamberlain Hastings, a longtime ally of King Edward even before he won the crown, because "she thought him secretly familiar with the King in wanton company." Shakespeare picks up this theme in Richard's advice that Hastings should "give Mistress Shore one gentle kiss the more," referring to Jane Shore, onetime mistress of Edward IV and then of Hastings.

Given the status of Hastings as Lord Chamberlain and lifelong friend and key adviser of King Edward IV, his support would be important for Richard's plans. Despite the warnings from Lord Stanley to fly to the north ("Tell him his fears are shallow," Hastings says to Stanley's messenger), the Lord Chamberlain agrees to Richard's summons to a meeting of the Council, allegedly to discuss arrangements for the coronation of King Edward's son. The Lord Chamberlain's fate is sealed, however, when he tells Richard's messenger, Catesby, that rather than have Richard get the crown, "I'll have this crown of mine cut from my shoulders." This is exactly what happens in act 3, scene 4, when Richard turns on his brother's old ally and accuses him of treachery.

Hastings is quickly dispatched, and Buckingham and Richard tell the Lord Mayor of London that Hastings had just been discovered planning to murder both of them. Richard tells the Mayor, "I would have had you heard the traitor speak, and timorously confess the manner and purpose of his treasons." However, "the loving haste of these our friends," has meant that Hastings has already met his fate. The Lord Mayor, seeing how the wind is blowing, says of Hastings, "he deserved his death." Somewhat later, a scrivener – a professional scribe – appears with the indictment of Hastings; Richard's man Catesby had the project begun the night before, hours before the alleged treason was discovered. "Bad is the world," the scrivener observes. Holinshed says the proclamation of Hastings's treachery was so carefully prepared and produced on such short notice "that every child might well perceive that it was prepared before."

Building Support

London was the economic center of the nation, and the support of its merchants and artisans was critical to the success of a king's reign. Edward IV had relentlessly cultivated Londoners; and Richard, too, now seeks their approval, sending Buckingham to recruit them to his side by making two attacks on Edward – first to "infer the bastardy of Edward's children" because Edward supposedly had a prior contract of marriage before he wed Elizabeth Woodville – and second to say that Edward was not really the son of the duke of York because he was supposedly conceived while the duke was engaged in wars in France. Richard has the delicacy to tell Buckingham that in terms of this last charge, "Yet touch this sparingly, as if t'were far off, because, my lord, you know my mother lives." In Holinshed, this news is broken by a clergyman, a Dr. Shaw, in a sermon at St. Paul's Cross.

In the play, the woman is identified as a Lady Elizabeth Lucy. The prior contract of marriage, if true, was a serious issue. A troth-plight or pledge of this kind had the legal weight of marriage, making Edward's marriage to Elizabeth Woodville essentially bigamous, and their children thus illegitimate.

Buckingham's first attempt to kick off a popular demand for Richard to take the throne comes to very little. The story comes from Holinshed. After a spirited address by him on Richard's behalf, the assembled multitude "spake not a word, but like dumb statues or breathing stones, stared each on other, and looked deadly pale," Buckingham tells Richard. After a small claque Buckingham had brought along shouted "God save King Richard," says Buckingham, he told the crowd, "This general applause and cheerful shout argues your wisdoms and love of Richard," and he left.

He has a second chance, however, when the Mayor and a group of leading citizens approach, and Buckingham and Richard cook up a scheme. When the Lord Mayor and the Aldermen arrive, Buckingham tells them Richard is unavailable. Unlike the late King Edward, Buckingham says, Richard is "not dallying with a brace of courtesans, but meditating with two deep divines . . . to enrich his watchful soul." Richard appears, flanked by two clergymen, to speak briefly with his guests. Buckingham speaks for them all, demanding that Richard agree to become king. After a show of considerable reluctance ("my desert unmeritable shuns your high request"), Richard agrees to take the crown.

By act 4, scene 2, Richard is wearing the crown, and the acting is over. He tells Buckingham, "Young Edward lives. Think now what I would speak." When Buckingham fails to grasp the obvious, Richard jumps in, saying, "Shall I be plain? I wish the bastards dead, and I would have it suddenly performed." Buckingham, Richard's closest confidant and right arm, finally balks. After he leaves, Richard says that Buckingham "no more shall be the neighbor to my counsels," while Sir James Tyrrel is more than willing to deal with Richard's "two deep enemies, foes to my rest and my sweet sleep's disturbers." Tyrrel says to Richard, "Let me have open means to come to them, and soon I'll rid you from the fear of them." According to Holinshed, Richard turned to Tyrrel not after Buckingham refused him, but rather after he sent a John Greene to the Tower to tell officials there that the princes were to be executed. Sir Robert Brakenbury, Constable of the Tower, refused, and

Richard then turned to Tyrrel, arranging for him to get the keys from Brakenbury.

On Buckingham's return, he asks the king for something Richard had promised him before his elevation, the earldom of Hereford. Richard's reply – "I am not in the giving vein today" – is enough to remind Buckingham of one of the deaths he helped Richard engineer, that of Lord Hastings, the former Lord Chamberlain, who crossed Richard but once. Buckingham decides to flee for Wales "while my fearful head is on."

Tyrrel tells the audience that the princes are dead, "the most arch deed of piteous massacre," before Richard arrives, and he tells the king only that he has done "the thing you gave in charge." Richard is obviously pleased but too busy to hear the details. He tells Tyrrel to come to him after supper, "When thou shalt tell me the process of their death. Meantime, but think how I may do thee good." On the news that her sons are dead, Queen Elizabeth says, "Wilt thou, Oh God, fly from such gentle lambs. . . . When didst thou sleep when such a deed was done?"

Richard determines that the only way to assure his continuance on the throne is to marry his niece Elizabeth, daughter of King Edward IV and Elizabeth Woodville (Richard's wife Anne had died early in 1485 CE). In a reprise of his wooing of Lady Anne, he apologizes to the queen for the deaths of her brothers and her children. Richard says, "What is done cannot now be amended; men shall deal unadvisedly sometimes," and persuades the queen to bring his suit before her daughter. According to Holinshed, however, it was Richard's messengers, "men both of wit and gravity, so persuaded the Queen with great and pregnant reasons."

The news comes that Henry Tudor, the earl of Richmond, is on the move from his base in France. Meanwhile, rebellion is everywhere, including one led by Buckingham. Richard is distraught until better news arrives – Buckingham's army is dispersed and Richmond has turned back to France; then a mixture of good news and bad – Buckingham has been apprehended, but Richmond has finally landed. Richard takes the field, saying, "While we reason here, a royal battle might be won and lost."

Buckingham is executed, and Richard pulls together his forces. The night before the battle of Bosworth, Richard is troubled by dreams: visitations from the men he has killed, from Prince Edward and Henry VI to his brother George, the Woodville relations of the Queen, Hastings, Buckingham and the princes in the Tower. "Oh coward conscience, how does thou afflict me!" says Richard. Meanwhile, Richmond, on the other side of the field, enjoys "the sweetest sleep, and fairest-boding dreams, that ever entr'ed in a drowsy head."

In his oration to his soldiers Richmond describes Richard as "a bloody tyrant and a homicide," and says Richard's troops "had rather have us win than him they follow." In his own speech to his followers, Richard calls Richmond "a paltry fellow . . . a milksop" and his soldiers from Brittany "these overweening rags of France, these famished beggars, weary of their lives . . ." ("Beggarly Bretons and fainthearted Frenchmen" is how Richard describes them in Holinshed's account.)

Richard suspected the loyalty of Lord Stanley, nominally on his side but the stepfather of the earl of Richmond; he had insisted that Stanley's son be left with the royal household as a hostage. In fact, Stanley's decision to come in on Richmond's side swings the battle to the rebels.

Accounts of the battle say that Richard tried to attack Richmond directly but was surrounded by troops from the other side and eventually cut down. Shakespeare has him calling for a horse, not to flee at the recommendation of one of his aides, but to go in search of Richmond, who arrives and kills him. Richard's crown, found supposedly under a hedge, is placed on Richmond's head. The new king, as a representative of the Lancasters, pledges to "unite the White Rose and the Red" or Lancaster and York by marrying Elizabeth, daughter of the Yorkist Edward IV, thus bringing to a close the long civil war during which "England hath long been mad and scarred herself . . . now civil wounds are stopped, peace lives again."

Henry Tudor, as Henry VII, ruled from 1485 to 1509 CE. After his wife Elizabeth of York died in 1503 CE, he never remarried. Henry VII had to deal with two pretenders to the throne, who were sponsored by dissident elements in the nobility. Lambert Simnel claimed to be the son of the duke of Clarence; Perkin Warbeck pretended to be the younger of the two princes who met their fate in the Tower. Simnel ended up working in the royal kitchens; Warbeck was executed after an escape attempt. Henry VII's heir was Arthur, Prince of Wales, but Arthur died in 1502 CE. At Henry VII's death, the crown was passed to Arthur's younger brother, who was crowned Henry VIII.

The Princes in the Tower

The most compelling evidence of Richard III's villainy is the death of the princes in the Tower of London. But how strong is the evidence that Richard had his nephews murdered? The circumstantial evidence certainly points to Richard, but there is a body of thought that says the evidence also can point to other suspects.

The primary source for the belief that it was Richard comes from Sir James Tyrrel, who confessed to the crime more than twenty years later before he was executed by Henry VII's authorities for an unrelated crime. The long period of silence and some inconsistencies in the story raise issues of credibility. In the seventeenth century, two skeletons were discovered buried in a chest inside the Tower, skeletons examined in the twentieth century and identified as that of a thirteen-year-old and a ten-year-old, which would certainly fit the ages of the princes concerned. But it is impossible to date the skeletons accurately with current technology. If they are those of the princes, it would throw into doubt one alternate story about their deaths – that they were spirited out of the Tower and died later.

Henry VII is one candidate for the villain of this piece because the princes, if they survived until his victory in 1485 CE, posed a great threat to his throne. Among the adherents of this theory was the English mystery writer Josephine Tey, whose book, *The Daughter of Time*, explores this theory.

Who else would have profited from the boys' deaths? One answer is the duke of Buckingham. Buckingham had his own claim to the throne, based on a long pedigree of parents, grandparents, and great-grandparents who were daughters, younger sons, and cousins of the royal line. Although tenuous, his claim was certainly no worse than that of Henry Tudor. Tudor's descent from Henry V's queen was irregular at best, because Queen Catherine and Owen Tudor may not have been married at all under English law; Tudor's mother was a Beaufort, a descendant of John of Gaunt and his mistress, Catherine Swynford, legitimized only after the death of Gaunt's legal wife. Buckingham's ambition may have been unrealistic, but the princes stood in his way as much as in Richard's.

For Further Viewing

Richard III is one of Shakespeare's most popular plays, and there have been a number of movie versions. The classic is that of Laurence Olivier, whose 1955 film presents Richard as fascinating and repellent at the same time. Ian McKellen plays Richard III in a 1995 version directed by Richard Loncraine and set in a fascist twentieth-century Britain; the outstanding cast also includes Annette Bening, Jim Broadbent, and Maggie Smith. *Looking for Richard* is Al Pacino's 1996 film of his attempt to make a movie of the play; it includes a number of completed scenes and much discussion with the cast about the text and its interpretation. Besides Pacino as Richard III, the cast includes Kevin Spacey, Alec Baldwin, Winona Ryder, and Estelle Parsons.

9

"These fierce vanities"

Henry VIII

The preceding play, *Richard III*, ended with Richard's defeat by Henry Tudor, who became King Henry VII. After having dramatized every reign for nearly a century, Shakespeare elected not to create a play about Henry VII's rule. However, Henry Tudor's son, who came to power in 1509 CE as Henry VIII, proved irresistible as a dramatic subject. Henry was the second son of Henry VII and Queen Elizabeth of York and had been headed for a career in the church, a common repository for the well-educated younger sons of noble families. But his older brother Arthur died in 1502 CE, and Henry ended up on the throne.

England and Its Continental Rivals

The most important geopolitical players at the time were France, centrally located in Western Europe, populous, and relatively prosperous; and Spain, a maritime power beginning to profit enormously from the gold and silver of its conquests in the New World. (Those funds might have come to England if the famously parsimonious Henry VII had taken up the Columbus family on their request for sponsorship of their explorations, a request they later made, successfully, to Ferdinand and Isabel of Spain.)

England's closest – and most complicated – relationship was with France. The Hundred Years' War between the two countries (which lasted longer than a century but was in fact an on-and-off conflict) had effectively drawn to a close before Henry VIII took the throne, but relations between the nations were still complex. Henry's sister, for instance, was briefly the queen of France before her elderly husband, Louis XII, died. And Henry, at least officially, had not given up the English claims to France that had kept the Hundred Years' War going. He often styled himself king of France as well as of England.

The Queen from Spain

Arthur's marriage to the daughter of the Spanish king, one of the most powerful men in Europe, was an attempt to balance the geopolitical power game by strengthening England's ties to France's competitor. On Arthur's death, Henry married her. Despite biblical injunctions against a man marrying a woman who had been his brother's wife, maintaining the alliance and keeping the lady's very substantial dowry in England argued for the marriage. A papal dispensation was sought and granted in 1503 CE, although the marriage did not take place until after Henry's accession.

The partnership between Henry and Catherine lasted for some twenty years. In its early days, Henry had relied on the queen for advice and help in running the country. It was she who was left in charge when he went on his first campaign to France, and while Henry was winning a small and indecisive battle there, English forces, at least nominally in her charge, won a far more important strategic victory over Scottish rebels at Flodden Field near the Scottish border.

The queen had borne seven children, but all the sons were stillborn or died in infancy, despite the care lavished on them by the royal household. The lack of a son was a very important political matter for the nation. Given the history of usurpations and coups of the previous century, including the interminable Wars of the Roses, ensuring a smooth succession was a vital matter for the peace of the realm.

Henry VIII

The image that has come down to us of Henry VIII, encouraged by his famous, swaggering portrait by the court painter Hans Holbein, is of a self-indulgent, imperious monarch, trailing a string of wives, two of them without their heads. But the young Henry VIII presents quite a different picture.

While his father had been a man of modest stature, Henry hearkened back to his mother's father, his grandfather on the Yorkist side, King Edward IV. Like him, Henry was well over six feet tall, an unusual height for the period, and a first-class athlete. He was one of the best horsemen in his kingdom, could outshoot his best archers, and excelled at all physical games. His court featured some of the best music in Europe, and he was an amateur musician of some ability, writing mass settings and secular songs. His father had been known for his thrift, but Henry loved luxury and display. He became famous across Europe for his extravagance in clothes and furnishings. He was also very well educated, spoke several languages, and was a particular student of theology. He was by reliable accounts very good-looking and thoroughly charming. He was also, when he came to the throne, only eighteen years old.

For a new king as strong-minded as Henry, the first task would be to form his own administration. To continue with the advisers who had served his father would be to fail to put his own stamp on the kingdom. But there were only a limited number of available men with the knowledge and talent to help administer a nation. Thus, while retaining some of his father's key aides, Henry began promoting an able and extremely hard-working churchman who had served his father in a number of important, if not critical, roles.

Thomas Wolsey

Wolsey had risen from ordinary, even modest circumstances. His father was an innkeeper and cattle dealer in the port town of Ipswich, on the North Sea. (Wolsey's enemies described his father as a butcher, prompting the duke of Buckingham's description of Wolsey in act 1 as "that butcher's cur.") An intellectual prodigy, Wolsey was sent in his teens from the local school to Oxford, where he attained a degree at the age of fifteen – several years younger than was usual – and was dubbed the "boy bachelor." He became part of the faculty and administration at Oxford, showing an aptitude in particular for building projects, a concern that would occupy him for most of his life.

The Roman Catholic Church's near-monopoly on education meant that men of the middle and lower classes who had an interest in academics or administration – such as Wolsey – could most easily fulfill their ambitions by joining the clergy. Such men took holy orders as a career move, rather than from any strong religious impulse. In fact, many senior administrative posts in the English administration at this time were filled by career bureaucrats who were also churchmen and who were paid out of church funds, from the parishes or bishoprics around the country to which the king had assigned them. (They stayed in London or Westminster; their pastoral duties were performed by vicars or other delegates.)

Wolsey had begun his career as a parish priest, but such duties suited neither his inclinations nor his talents. He got an appointment to the staff of the leading churchman in the country, the Archbishop of Canterbury, then joined the household of the governor of Calais, the port on the French side of the English Channel that was then an English possession. Wolsey's ability and industry eventually recommended him into the royal household, and he became a mid-level bureaucrat for King Henry VII. By the accession of Henry VIII, Wolsey had a proven reputation as an effective administrator. In addition, as a commoner,

Wolsey was not identified with or tied to any noble group and would owe his allegiance completely to his sponsor and patron, Henry VIII.

Wolsey had one more significant advantage. He was willing to do most of the hard work it would take to actually run the country, leaving the king to occupy himself with the natural inclinations of a rich and healthy eighteen-year-old: sports, popular music, and romance. And although Wolsey was about twenty years older than the King, he was tireless.

Such was Wolsey's efficiency that in the early years of his reign the king put more and more trust in him, and he was granted broad powers in civil government, along with church offices, including a Cardinal's hat. It was Wolsey who met first with foreign ambassadors, and it was Wolsey who maintained a voluminous correspondence – often in his own name – with foreign powers. According to some authorities, letters that were sufficiently important to be sent in the king's own hand were written out first by Wolsey and then dispatched to the king. Henry, who found tedious the task of composing state documents, would then copy them out in his own handwriting.

The Field of the Cloth of Gold

Wolsey played a role in organizing and supplying some of Henry VIII's Continental military adventures, but the first real triumph of his organizing genius was in 1520 CE, when he arranged a meeting between Henry VIII and his French counterpart, the equally young and ambitious Francis I. Legions of knight and retainers, headed by their respective monarchs, met near the coast of northern France for days of games, tournaments, and feasting. So lavish were the costumes and appointments that the affair was known as the Field of the Cloth of Gold, and it ended with loud pledges of mutual support and amity.

Wolsey made all the arrangements, attended with his own retainers, and hosted the most important meetings. He got the credit for the event's success and the displeasure of the nobles. Says Holinshed, "The peers of the realm . . . seemed to grudge that such a costly journey should be taken in hand to their importunate charges and expenses . . ." because they had to spend huge sums of their own to transport their troops and retainers to what turned out to be no more than a foreign coming-out party for their new sovereign.

The Play

Henry VIII opens with three lords complaining how much the meeting on the Field of the Cloth of Gold had cost, not to mention questioning Wolsey's role in the affair. On hearing a description of the pomp of the occasion, the duke of Buckingham asks, "[W]hat had he to do in these fierce vanities?" His unhappiness opens the play's subplot concerning his fate. The duke of Buckingham was one of the most popular and powerful nobles in the kingdom. Accused in the play (and in real life) of plotting to kill Henry and replace him on the throne, Buckingham was tried and executed. Holinshed reports that witnesses testified Buckingham said "that he would attain to the crown if King Henry should die without issue" and that if he thought he was to be arrested by King Henry VIII, "he would have played the part that his father had intended to put in practice against King Richard III . . . having a knife secretly about him he would have thrust it into the body of King Richard. . . ." Readers of the previous play will remember that *Richard III*'s duke of Buckingham, having helped Richard gain the throne, eventually turned against him and was executed for treason. *Henry VIII*'s duke of Buckingham was the son of the duke of Buckingham in *Richard III*. In part because Wolsey first brought the matter to the King's attention, many nobles believed the Cardinal had concocted the evidence to remove a popular rival.

The "Amicable" Loan

In 1525 CE, Wolsey met a major defeat. Henry was determined to go to war with France to take advantage of the recent defeat and capture of King Francis I by the Holy Roman Emperor Charles V. The problem was that he couldn't afford it, and parliament, which had in recent years been browbeaten into passing new taxes, was in no mood to go further. Henry needed to raise the necessary funds however he could, and the strategy – implemented if not created by Wolsey – involved a series of involuntary loans from nobles, cities, and other funding sources. The rate was set at one-sixth of total revenue, a sizable amount. While the official description of the process was that of an "amicable" loan, in fact there was virtually no amicability about it. Protests were widespread, and in the southeast of England there was virtually open rebellion. Henry and Wolsey eventually had to back down.

In the play, it is through the intercession of Queen Catherine that the tax is lifted. She brings Henry the news that the tax is fomenting unrest and that even the king "escapes not language unmannerly" that "almost appears in loud rebellion." Henry orders the tax lifted, and Wolsey, while complying, tells his clerk to make sure word is spread that this act of mercy is Wolsey's, not the king's. Holinshed says, "The Cardinal, to deliver himself of the evil will of the Commons . . . caused it to be bruised abroad that through his intercession the King had pardoned and released all things."

Obvious Luxury

A principal criticism of Wolsey's tenure was his love of lavish display. Even in a time when such display was a normal demonstration of rank and power, Wolsey was an extreme case, to the extent that he was thought to be – or at least lived like – the richest man in the realm. He was a great builder of private and public buildings, and his greatest effort was expended on his official residence, Hampton Court. It was said to have 1,000 rooms and as many servants, and Wolsey hosted lavish parties for the most important people in the kingdom.

The play dramatizes this side of Wolsey, making him the gracious host of a lavish gathering, kicking off the evening with a bowl of wine and the statement, "the lady or gentlemen who is not merry is no friend of mine." The king then arrives with a group of friends, all masked, who pretend to be French, and Henry notices the charms of Anne Boleyn (a bit of dramatic license, since in reality Henry had long been aware of her).

Wolsey's love of showing off his money and power was not confined to special events. According to contemporary accounts, his regular commute from Hampton Court to the Star Chamber in Westminster Palace was essentially a parade. He was preceded by a man carrying the Great Seal of England, a gentleman carrying his Cardinal's hat on a pillow, others bearing great silver crosses, and his "gentleman-ushers" crying out "make way for my Lord Cardinal." More noblemen and gentlemen followed, each bearing a gilt poleaxe, and each surrounded by his own footmen and servants. Wolsey wore robes of the finest satin and velvet and though, as befit a churchman, he rode not a horse but a mule, his saddle was velvet and his stirrups made of gold.

The Private Wolsey

Whatever his public virtues as a diplomat and an administrator, Woolsey in private was not a model churchman. While he was reasonably discreet, Wolsey for years kept a mistress by whom he had two children. The woman eventually married someone else, but Wolsey saw to the well-being of both children. His daughter became a nun and his son a priest and scholar. (In the play, the earl of Surrey is talking about this relationship when he berates the Cardinal about the time when the "wench lay kissing in your arms.")

The King's Great Matter

Wolsey's downfall was the result of his failure to acquire for Henry VIII the thing Henry came to want most – a papal annulment of his marriage to Catherine.

There is a popular image of Henry VIII as a man so driven by lust that he turns away from his dutiful wife of twenty years in order to marry the younger and more beautiful Anne Boleyn. In truth, sex was certainly part of Henry's makeup, but he didn't need a divorce or annulment to have it. Long before the potential annulment arose as an issue, Henry had other romantic interests. He had an illegitimate son, known as Henry Fitzroy, whom he openly embraced (but whose route to the throne would have been problematic, and who died in 1536 CE at the age of seventeen). Historians believe Henry knew the Boleyn family (called Bullen in the play) in part because he had already had an affair with Anne's sister, Mary. Absent his dynastic concerns, there is reason to think Henry might have contented himself with a simple affair that encompassed yet another member of the Boleyn household.

Wolsey's private attitude toward the king's plans to seek an annulment is not clear. But from Wolsey's perspective, if the royal union was legally dissolved, a marriage to a French noblewoman could strengthen the claim of the English king to the French throne, if not in Henry's case then for their son. (The play has Wolsey saying quite clearly, "We'll have no Bullens here.") Wolsey's candidate was the French king's sister, the Duchess of Alencon.

In any case, it fell to Wolsey to undertake a series of machinations to get the current pope, Clement VII, to agree that the dispensation granted by his predecessor was invalid, making the marriage to Catherine illegal from the beginning. This strategy led to a trial of the issue in England chaired by Wolsey and a papal representative.

The Trial

Catherine makes a moving defense of her honor in the play, embellished from Holinshed's historical record of the same speech. She accuses Wolsey of being her enemy – Holinshed says she "most grievously accused the cardinal of untruth, deceit, wickedness and malice . . . and thus she departed, without any further answer at that time or any other, and never would appear after in any court." Shakespeare also follows Holinshed in letting Wolsey ask the king to tell the assembly if in fact the cardinal was the instigator of the matter. The king replies that it was he himself who had fastened on the issue, and that Wolsey had inclined against it.

The play picks up Holinshed's account of a visit by Wolsey and the papal representative, Cardinal Campeius, to Catherine, and their attempt to persuade the Queen to return to the court or to let the king dispose of the matter according to his own desires. "The hearts of princes kiss obedience, so much they love it, but to stubborn spirits they swell and grow as terrible as storms," Wolsey tells her. Other chroniclers indicate that Wolsey paid more than one visit to

Catherine in an attempt to negotiate the issue, but she never returned to the court.

The trial went on for months and then the papal representative left without making a decision, precisely the result Henry did not want. After dragging the original royal marriage through this process – much of the testimony revolved around the question of whether Catherine's first marriage to Henry's brother had been consummated – the issue was back in the pope's hands. Says Holinshed, "this protracting of the conclusion of the matter, King Henry took most displeasantly."

Under normal circumstances, a favorable decision in such a matter would have been granted as a routine courtesy to a monarch like Henry, who had been supportive of papal initiatives and who was firmly in the Catholic rather than the Lutheran camp. But the hands of the pope were tied. He was effectively the prisoner of Queen Catherine's nephew and protector, Charles V, who had invaded and captured Rome.

Wolsey's Disgrace

There is a story in Holinshed of the fall of the Bishop of Winchester in the time of Henry VII. According to this account, the bishop, who apparently kept two sets of books, forgetfully told his clerk to send to the king the true set – the one that detailed his many thieveries and extortions. The mistake led, of course, to his dismissal. The play adopts the incident wholesale but applies it to Wolsey. It also adds a matter discussed in Holinshed – a letter Wolsey supposedly sent to the pope asking him to delay consideration of the annulment until Wolsey had made sure that the king would not turn around and marry Anne Boleyn rather than Wolsey's much more diplomatic candidate, the sister of the French king.

In the play, Henry engages the cardinal in a dialogue about loyalty before putting the offending papers in his hands. The occasion provides an opportunity for Wolsey's soliloquy on his fate: "This paper has undone me. 'Tis the account of all that world of wealth I have drawn together for mine own ends. . . . I have touched the highest point of all my greatness, and from that full meridian of my glory I haste now to my setting."

The anger of the noble families at Wolsey is a continuing element in the drama, but the play sums it up in a scene derived from Holinshed that shows the dukes of Norfolk and Suffolk, the earl of Surrey, and the Lord Chamberlain attempting to retrieve from Wolsey the Great Seal, the sign of his civil office, after his disgrace. They make their fears and resentments of the provincial upstart clear, accusing him of plotting Buckingham's fall, along with "gleaning all the land's wealth into one, into your own hands . . . by extortion," Given Wolsey's contempt of the nobility, they fear that their sons, if Wolsey continues his efforts "will scarce be gentlemen."

Historically, it was because of the failure of the papal strategy that Wolsey found himself stripped of most of his offices and turned out of his palace at Hampton Court. As a sign that the king had not completely turned his back on him, Wolsey was eventually allowed to move to the north of England to his see as Archbishop of York.

While the play does not deal with this later period, it does include a scene with his aide Thomas Cromwell that takes place before Wolsey's banishment. Wolsey talks about what a relief he has found in his disgrace: "Never so truly happy. . . . I feel within a peace above all earthly dignities, a still and quiet conscience," describing his former state as "a burden too heavy for a man who hopes for heaven."

Wolsey's episcopal efforts in York were not to last long. Letters, forged or authentic, appeared in London that in Wolsey's name sought the help of the French king in restoring the cardinal to his position and scheming against the marriage to Anne. On Henry's orders, a party left for York to take Wolsey into custody in November, 1530 CE, and convey him to the Tower of London. No one – least of all Wolsey himself – expected he would emerge alive. But fate intervened. Wolsey's health had been failing for some time. On the road to London, a slow passage given Wolsey's condition, the party came to the Abbey of St. Mary of the Meadows in Leicester. "Father Abbot, I have come to lay my bones among you," an exhausted Wolsey told his host, according to Holinshed. He died there a few days later.

In Holinshed's account, it is on his deathbed that Wolsey says, "if I had served God as diligently as I have done the king, he would not have given me over in my gray hairs." The play's version of this conversation comes much earlier in Wolsey's life and is a good deal more poetic: "Oh, Cromwell, Cromwell, if I had but served my God with half the zeal I served my king, he would not in my age have left me naked to my enemies."

The Rise of Cranmer

After the play's last view of Wolsey, the drama goes on to cover a contest between orthodox bishops and Henry's chosen successor for Wolsey as leading churchman, the reformist (and suspected Lutheran) Thomas Cranmer. Cranmer is about to be sent to the Tower for spreading, in the words of the Lord Chancellor, "new opinions, diverse and dangerous; which are heresies, and not reformed, may prove pernicious." The story of Cranmer's hearing before the Council on charges of heresy is not from Holinshed, but from John Foxe's *Book of Martyrs*, including the part where he brings out the king's signet ring and Foxe says of his accusers, "Upon the receipt of the King's token, they all rose and carried to the King his ring, surrendering that matter. . . ."

The play closes with the baptism of Anne and Henry's daughter, Princess Elizabeth, including a lengthy panegyric by Cranmer on how blessed England will be under her eventual leadership. (The lady in question, as Queen Elizabeth, had died less than a decade before the play was written, and her forty-year reign would have been fondly remembered by most of the audience.)

Henry's marriage to Anne Boleyn kicked off his marital soap opera. Anne went to the scaffold, while Henry married Jane Seymour, who died in childbirth; Anne of Cleves, whom he divorced; Catherine Howard, the scaffold again; and Katherine Parr, who survived him.

After Wolsey's downfall, the king was heard to complain that he could find no one who was as efficient and effective as Wolsey had been, but he never again permitted one individual to hold the reins of both church and state. Wolsey's successor as chancellor was the noted lawyer Thomas More, later executed for refusing to countenance Henry's setting himself up as head of the English church. Thomas Cranmer, Wolsey's successor as leading churchman and a featured character in the play's later scenes, was executed by Henry's daughter, Mary.

The final mention of Wolsey in the play neatly captures the ambiguities of his character and tenure. Catherine continued to live in England after the annulment, as the dowager princess of Wales (her first husband Arthur's title). As she lies dying, her gentleman-in-waiting, Griffith, brings her the news of Wolsey's passing (in fact, it had happened in 1530 CE, six years before Catherine's death in 1536 CE). Catherine details Wolsey's faults and says, "His promises were as he was then, mighty; but his performance, as he is now, nothing." Griffith, noting that "men's evil manners live in brass, their virtues we write in water," says of Wolsey that his overthrow "heaped happiness upon him . . . and he died fearing God."

Wolsey's Character

There are a number of contemporary sources for our view of Wolsey. Holinshed's *Chronicles* are often highly critical of him, but balancing them is Wolsey's much more sympathetic biography by his secretary, George Cavendish. While Cavendish's book was not printed until 1641 CE, manuscript copies were in circulation decades earlier, and to the extent Wolsey is sometimes shown in a more favorable light in the play, it may have been due to Shakespeare consulting sources who were familiar with Cavendish's biography.

One of the most telling details of Wolsey's character is his attitude toward religious dissenters. At this time, the English church was constantly burning books deemed heretical or doctrinally dangerous, a tactic Wolsey supported (Henry VIII's disagreement with the church was jurisdictional, not doctrinal). However, Wolsey "would burn books but not men," complained the strictly orthodox. His successor as Lord Chancellor, the sainted Thomas More, may have been a man for all seasons, but he did not share Wolsey's delicate sensibilities on this issue. More had no compunction about burning heretics who would not recant.

Wolsey had commissioned an elaborate tomb for himself, but his remains were interred at the abbey where he died. The tomb stayed empty for nearly two hundred years, until it was used as the base for the funeral monument for another lowborn provincial boy who had served his Crown. Horatio Nelson, hero of Trafalgar, the decisive naval battle that turned back the French tide in the Napoleonic wars, was buried in Wolsey's tomb.

History as Drama

The trial to determine the religious legality of Henry and Catherine's marriage was at Blackfriars, a Dominican abbey outside London. The location includes a specifically Shakespearian irony. By the time of the play's writing, about 1610 CE, the great hall at Blackfriars had become a theater, leased by Shakespeare's acting company, the King's Men. There is no record of *Henry VIII* having been performed in the smaller Blackfriars hall, for which Shakespeare is believed to have composed some of his later, intimate plays like *The Tempest* and *The Winter's Tale*. But it is hard to imagine that the company would not have been interested in staging the trial scene at the site where the trial had actually occurred some seventy years before.

For Further Viewing

The play – often with a focus on its opportunities for pageantry – was a staple of the English stage in the eighteenth and nineteenth centuries. It was revived for the coronation of Queen Elizabeth in the mid-1950s. The BBC version, shot in surviving Tudor interiors in 1979, has Timothy West as Wolsey, and features a remarkable performance by Claire Bloom as Catherine of Aragon.

Even if not always in Shakespeare's words, the story of Henry VIII is a tale often told. Notable modern versions of events from the life of Henry VIII include *A Man for All Seasons*, directed by Fred Zinneman and starring Paul Scofield. The 1966 film, based on Robert Bolt's play, tells the story of Wolsey's successor, Sir Thomas More. Orson Welles, whose physical bulk matches the surviving portraits of Wolsey in middle age, plays a brief role as the cardinal in the film's early moments. The film was remade for television in

1988 with Charlton Heston as More, John Gielgud as Wolsey, and Vanessa Redgrave, who had a cameo role as Anne Boleyn in the first film, promoted to More's wife Alice in the second.

Another popular retelling of some of these events, focusing on Anne Boleyn, is the 1969 film *Anne of the Thousand Days*, based on the Maxwell Anderson stage play. Geneviève Bujold plays the title role, while Richard Burton is Henry VIII and Anthony Quayle as Wolsey.

The national cable channel Showtime broadcast its own Henry VIII series in 2007, with Sam Neill as Wolsey and Jonathan Rhys Meyers as Henry.

Afterword

Our enjoyment of Shakespeare is enriched by
a knowledge of his sources. But his sources are
rewarding even without their connection to the
bard. Plutarch, Dio Cassius, Holinshed, and Hall
are still consulted by any serious student of these
periods; even when their accounts have been updated
(or even contradicted) by later scholars, their work
has created the prisms through which we view these
times and events.

Shakespeare seems to have read Plutarch in an
English version of a French translation of the original
Greek. We have the advantage of a number of more
recent translations. The one supervised by the
English poet and dramatist John Dryden, in the late
seventeenth century is the most poetic. More modern
versions, however, can be more accessible.

Holinshed and Hall are available in updated
editions and, to a certain extent, on the Internet. Some
editions of the plays now include selections from these
historians who served as Shakespeare's guides.

An excellent modern overview of Rome during the late republic is available in audio form from The Teaching Company, and there are dozens of books on the life of Julius Caesar and that of his heir Octavian, later known as Augustus. For the English plays, the biographies published as part of the Yale English Monarchs series are particularly useful, along with the very readable works about the Wars of the Roses and Henry VIII by Alison Weir.

INDEX